THE CHINESE,

THEIR PRESENT AND FUTURE: MEDICAL,
POLITICAL, AND SOCIAL.

A Gentleman in Winter Dress.

THE CHINESE,

THEIR PRESENT AND FUTURE: MEDICAL, POLITICAL, AND SOCIAL.

BY

ROBERT COLTMAN, Jr.

Illustrated

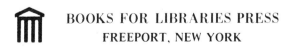

BOOKS FOR LIBRARIES PRESS
FREEPORT, NEW YORK

First Published 1891
Reprinted 1972

Library of Congress Cataloging in Publication Data

Coltman, Robert, 1862-1931.
    The Chinese, their present and future: medical,
political, and social.

    ([BCL/select bibliographies reprint series])
    Reprint of the 1891 ed.
    1. China--Social life and customs. 2. Hygiene,
Public--China. I. Title.
DS709.C73 1972   915.1'03   72-4164
ISBN 0-8369-6874-3

TO

MY MOTHER AND FATHER

THIS VOLUME

IS

AFFECTIONATELY DEDICATED.

THE AUTHOR.

PREFACE.

SINCE my return to the United States, last spring, I have met many friends, in and out of the medical profession, who have at various times pressed me to write my experiences in China, and my views of the present situation there and future prospects of the country. I have tried in the following pages to present, in the briefest form possible, the answers to questions constantly asked me. The illustrations are all from photographs in my own collection, most of them taken by myself. As I have resided and traveled only in North China, the reader will understand that my descriptions apply to the people living north of Shanghai, unless explicitly stated otherwise.

ROBERT COLTMAN, JR.

411 PINE STREET, PHILADELPHIA,
December 1, 1891.

TABLE OF CONTENTS.

PAGE

PREFACE, ... V

INTRODUCTION, ... 1
  Interest in the race excited. Commissioned to China. Japan. Nearing
  Shanghai. Shanghai in summer. Arrival at Chefoo. Disgusted with
  sights and odors.

CHAPTER I.
FIRST IMPRESSIONS, ... 13
  Change of name. First lesson in Chinese. A ramble down hill. Diet of
  resident foreigners. Society of Chefoo. Chinese theatre. Onward.

CHAPTER II.
EN ROUTE TO THE INTERIOR, ... 27
  Looking for a steamer. On the ocean again. Passenger with cholera.
  Stuck in the river. How to settle a fare. Tientsin. Waiting for an
  escort. A house-boat. Up the Grand Canal. Arrival at Ssu Nü Ssu.
  Overland journey. Donkey-riding. A Chinese inn. Wheelbarrow-
  riding. Mobbed at Yü Cheng. Crossing the flooded farms. Crossing
  the Yellow River. Arrival at Chinanfu.

CHAPTER III.
AN INTERIOR CITY, ... 47
  City-gates. Lake in the city. Shops on the great street. Exchange of
  silver. The Governor's yamen. Coffins and monuments. Beggars.
  Population. Chinese Mohammedans. The Pao T'ou Ch'uan fair.

CHAPTER IV.
VISITING THE PEASANTRY, ... 61
  Starting to Chi Yang. Will not hear advice. A head in the basket. A
  primitive ferry. Two criminals. A mat inn in winter, No seclusion.
  My pants ridiculed. Arrival at our destination. Sympathy from an
  old lady. Entertained by Mr. Li. Village life. Change to native
  costume.

CHAPTER V.
CHARACTERISTICS OF THE NORTHERN CHINESE, . . . 80
  Size. Pride. Desire for male children. Mothers-in-law. Coolie life.
  Endurance. Swindling. Procrastination. Imitation. Crimes.

CHAPTER VI.
HOME LIFE, ... 94
  Three classes. Tao T'ai Chang; his residence. Rules for women. Con-
  cubinage. Ladies' costumes. Sociability. Banquets. Chinese deli-
  cacies. A middle-class family. Imposition in marriage contracts.
  Laboring class.

(vii)

PAGE

CHAPTER VII.

DISSIPATIONS,　　.　　.　　.　　.　　.　　.　　.　　.　　. 113

The social evil. Difference of opinion between Chinese and Japanese. Story of Judge Kuo. Novel sale. A missionary in trouble. Wines. Opium. Anti-opium pills.

CHAPTER VIII.

DISEASES PREVALENT IN CHINA,　.　　.　　.　　.　　.　　. 131

Dyspepsia; its causes. Eye diseases. Lung diseases. Leucocythemia. Stricture of the œsophagus. Ulcerations. The fevers of China. Dysentery; different forms; treatment of each. Demoniacal possession. Nervous diseases. Goitre. Surgery. Lack of Obstetricians.

CHAPTER IX.

LEPROSY,　　.　　.　　.　　.　　.　　.　　.　　.　　.　　. 155

Contagiousness. Ancient literature on the subject. Story from Book of Marvels. Female immunity. Typical cases. Treatment of Leprosy. Syphilis. Other venereal diseases.

CHAPTER X.

MISSIONARIES AND THEIR WORK,　　.　　.　　.　　.　　. 169

Who are they? Criticism upon them. Methods of work. Medical work. Eminent medical men in the ranks. Educational work. Native clergy.

CHAPTER XI.

BUSINESS OPPORTUNITIES,　　.　　.　　.　　.　　.　　.　　. 179

Circumstances of the population. Foreigners restricted to the ports. Language a necessity. Railroads badly needed. Viceroy Li in favor of railroads. Lines first needed. Articles salable and unsalable. Effect of the exclusion bill.

CHAPTER XII.

PRESENT POLITICAL SITUATION,　.　　.　　.　　.　　.　　. 191

Government outlined. Squeezing. Civil service a fraud. Hatred toward foreigners; its cause. Condition of the army and navy. Possible enemies. Riots and their consequences. Proclamation of the Tsung Li Yamen.

CHAPTER XIII.

FUTURE PROSPECTS,　　.　　.　　.　　.　　.　　.　　.　　. 205

China overcrowded. Emigration beyond Asia not a necessity. Mines unworked. Manufactures not encouraged. People discontented. Ability to defend her borders. Immediate action necessary.

THE CHINESE,

THEIR PRESENT AND FUTURE: MEDICAL, POLITICAL, AND SOCIAL.

INTRODUCTION.

For four years I had been reading the journals of the various societies employing medical men as missionaries abroad. Africa, Siam, Korea, India, and China all at first claimed a share of my attention, but at last I became so interested in the latter country that I could not pass a laundry in the city of Philadelphia without stopping to watch the almond-eyed Celestial use his mouth as an atomizer and spray to perfection the shirt-front, destined to be speedily ironed and polished to a degree unattainable by the daughters of Erin, whom he was fast displacing. I used to wonder if the internal construction of his larynx and pharynx corresponded with that of the Caucasian race, with which I was familiar as a student of anatomy. Then I would become absorbed in reflections on the peculiarity of his dress, color of his skin, the shape of his eyes, his apparently guttural dialect, his pertinacity in retaining the queue and native style of wearing-apparel in a foreign country, where it excited so much ridicule, etc., etc., until finally I would meander off, only to stop and go through a second series of similar reflections upon seeing another shop kept by one of this peculiar race. My interest constantly deepening, I determined to read all available literature on the subject, and with that end in

view secured all the works on China I could obtain, and
for some time my leisure hours were pleasantly spent in
this interesting study; but early in my quest for information I perceived a lack of detail and meagreness of
description, especially in regard to the social state of the
people and country at present, which was anything but
satisfying.   Suddenly one day came the thought, " Why
not go and see them in their own country and make a
study of them?   If it is true, as stated, that they have
no properly educated physicians, my medical training
and experience could not but be a key to their acquaintance, perhaps friendship, besides being the means of
doing much good to the afflicted unable to secure skilled
assistance."   After considerable discussion of the pros
and cons of this subject, and some opposition at first
from my wife, I in the end decided to make application
to the American Presbyterian Board of Foreign Missions
to accept my services as a physician on their staff in
China.

The proper credentials were demanded as to my
graduation from a recognized medical college, and also
as to my standing in the profession and Christian character.   These being considered satisfactory, I was notified
that I was commissioned a medical missionary physician,
and directed to proceed to the station of Chinanfu, the
capital city of the province of Shantung, in North China.
On April 8, 1885, I received my commission, and on the
21st of May my wife, infant son, and self took passage
from San Francisco on the Pacific mail-steamer *Rio de
Janeiro*, Captain Cobb, for Yokohama, Japan, *en route*
to far Cathay.

The voyage across the Pacific Ocean has been the
subject of so many descriptions that I will not weary the

reader with a repetition; suffice it to state that we took the southern route, and visited the beautiful Hawaiian (better known as the Sandwich) Islands, and enjoyed the pleasure of spending one delightful day in the tropical city of Honolulu. This was the only day of the entire journey my wife was not seasick. From the Sandwich Islands we sailed north again, and west, arriving at the city of Yokohama on the morning of Friday, June 12th, having been twenty-two days out from San Francisco.

We were, of course, delighted with Japan—everybody is. I have yet to meet a person who was disappointed with the country or its inhabitants. From the moment of landing at Yokohama until the moment of leaving Nagasaki, one is in perpetual change of pleasant scenes. We visited the curio-shops, silk-shops, and temples; bought canes, scrolls, screens, and cuff-buttons in a most reckless fashion,—for, really, you see so many beautiful things, and apparently so cheap, that you will buy as long as your finances stand it. Every one who comes to Japan goes away much poorer, and, of course, the country benefits by visitors who come to spend.

The most striking feature of the people seems to me to be their cleanliness. Everybody is clean ; everything is clean. I saw several pigs in Tokio, and, wonder of wonders! they were clean. A week passed by like lightning, and only one unpleasant incident in that time, which came in the form of a terrific earthquake that nearly shook us out of bed, on the night of June 14th, at Yokohama. Earthquakes may be pleasant when one gets used to them, but, after living for twenty odd years in the steady, young United States, a person is rather unfitted for the frisky gambols of hoary old Nippon. One short week of respite from the motion of

the ship, and our steamer is about to leave again. Hotel
bills are paid, trunks taken out to the steam-launch in
waiting, a run of half a mile in the launch, ascent of
companion-way of the Japanese company's steamer, and
again we are moving onward, westward, to the land of
Confucius, and to the most populous nation of the earth.

"What is that dark line ahead and to the right?"
I asked. "That, sir, is the coast of China, and if we
strike sufficient water on the bar you will be in Shanghai by noon," replied Captain Walker, of the Japanese
Mitsu Bishi steamer, *Nagoya Maru*, to whom I had addressed my question. We were just a week from Yokohama, Japan, and had met with rough weather all the
way, and now, though it had ceased raining, heavy
banks of storm-clouds still hung threateningly overhead,
and the June air was damp and close. "How far are
we from the land?" I ventured again. "Not more than
eight miles; you see, the land is very low here, and we
cannot see it until we are quite near. Ah! Doctor, I
pity you," continued the captain. "The idea of a young
man like you going into the interior of China to study
the natives, and dragging your wife along with you, too,
seems to me the height of foolishness. Why don't you
stop in Shanghai or Chefoo? There are plenty of natives in either of those places to satisfy you; and all
sorts, too. I see enough of them in Shanghai on one
trip to satisfy me forever,—the dirty, long-tailed heathen." "And, sir," said the mate, who was standing
by, "if you live to come back—which, of course, we
hope you will—you will be as yellow as one of those
fellows below there (pointing to a small group of Chinese deck-passengers huddled together on the main-deck

beneath us). We had, a few years ago, a nice young man come out with us as a passenger from the States, who was going with his wife to be a missionary to those heathen wretches; and when we took him home, two trips back, he was alone; buried his wife in China with small-pox; and he as yellow as saffron, and looking twenty years older; going home to die." "Do they all go home looking like that?" I asked, mentally questioning myself if I had not perhaps made a mistake in my determination to explore China. "Well, not all, but most of them," he replied, with a sort of sorrow in his voice. He could not truthfully say they were all broken-down wrecks. I commenced to recover. "Well, perhaps I may be one of those who won't go to pieces," I said. "Half-speed! Heave the lead!" called out the captain. "You see," he said, turning to me, "in this muddy-looking water we have no great depth, and the bottom is always shifting; so we have to take soundings every time we go in. Now, at Chefoo the vessels can all go in and come out, even large men-of-war, without sounding; but they have no river there to wash out the mud and silt it up in banks, as here." A little while later we were in sight of the signal-station of Woosung, anxiously looking with glasses to see if the tide-mark displayed would enable us to cross the bar. As we drew nearer we could see vessels of all nations, some lying inside and some outside the bar. On, on we go, closer and closer to the signal-station; but still the captain will not say whether he intends going over the bar or not, and all the passengers are becoming impatient, when the mate whispers to me, "This is the ' old man's' hobby. He'd sooner see a lot of impatient passengers than eat a good meal; but you can rest easy, Doctor. I think we will cross the bar; still, as the water is getting low and the tide running out, we will probably not go up more than five miles or so this morning. Then we will anchor, and, if in a hurry, you can take a sampan and go ashore; if not in a hurry, wait quietly on board until three or four o'clock, and with the incoming tide we will run up to the 'bund' (wharf)." It turned out just as the mate said, and in another hour we were dropping anchor about five miles below the wharf of the company, in midstream, as the low tide made farther advance risky. To stay quietly aboard until the tide changed was impossible to one of my temperament; so, after securing directions from the captain how to proceed, I called a sampan, deposited my wife, child, and valise therein, and pushed away from the *Nagoya* up stream.

The boatman worked lustily with his scull, heaving a sort of grunt, each time he swayed back and forth, that was not unmusical; but the tide was running swiftly out, and his utmost exertion made but slow progress. After an hour and a half of this (to foreigners) exasperatingly slow travel, during which we had gone about four miles, we spied some jinrickshaws at a wharf just ahead, and made our boatman pull in to the shore, in spite of his protestations that he was to take us to the steamboat-wharf. I paid him what I was told was the fare,—the sum of thirty cents Japanese money,—and he appeared satisfied; since, even though he had not carried us to the agreed point, he had received his full fare.

We were now surrounded by a lot of rickshaw-men, one of whom seized my valise, another my little boy, and the rest were crowding around my wife and self, jabbering such a lot of (to me) unmeaning chatter, that I was perfectly bewildered. "Tell them where you want to go, and ask them if they know where it is," said my clear-headed wife. "Oh, yes, of course. I say, do you know where No. 18 Peking Road is?" I asked the nearest Chinaman, who was trying to pull me toward his rickshaw. He replied in Chinese very volubly, but, of course, I did not understand a word. "Do you understand English?" I asked. Again an answer in that incomprehensible tongue. What to do was a question. Evidently, none of these men understood a word of English, but they would certainly take us into the European settlement, which we could see a mile away, and perhaps to a hotel, and then, of course, everything would be set straight. So, picking out the three cleanest rickshaws, we took seats therein, and pointed toward the settlement. Their owners at once grasped the miniature shafts, broke into a trot, and soon we were entering what appeared like a civilized country, or, rather, city ; and that, apparently, no small city either, for, as the men passed down the bund or river-front, we obtained some idea of the importance of the place as a business centre from the immense amount of shipping in the river. Ships of all nations, of every style of construction, so filled the river that skillful navigation was required in passing up or down stream. Rapidly passing numerous business houses of five and six stories in height, substantially and sometimes handsomely built, we suddenly turned a corner, our two-legged animals abruptly lowered their pulling end of the cart, and we were supposed to be at our destination. I read the sign, "Astor House," above the door-way, and concluded it must be a hotel, though it more resembled a large private residence.

Walking in through the door-way, I met a polite clerk, who, upon my informing him of my inability to make the rickshaw-men understand where to take me, kindly informed them, in what is known as pigeon English, that I desired to go to No. 18 Peking Road. After thanking him for his trouble, we were wheeled around, partly back over the same track, then a turn to the left, and after passing a few blocks farther we were taken into the large yard of the Presbyterian Mission Press, and warmly welcomed by Dr. and Mrs. Farnham, the genial superintendent and his wife.

We were now undoubtedly in China; that is, on Chinese soil; but Shanghai is, perhaps, the most cosmopolitan city on the face of the globe, for, although the Chinese predominate, the other nations of the earth all have their representatives. Germans, Portuguese, English, French, Americans, Danes, Italians, Parsees, and Ethiopians,—all are here; and the only man who excites any attention or surprise is some missionary from the interior, who, dressed in the native dress of China, with shaved head and queue, is sure to elicit a surprised and partly contemptuous smile from the native sons of China who pass him. We had evidently arrived at a bad time of the year to get a pleasant impression of Shanghai. The rainy season had commenced, and it was a time of moist heat, exceedingly trying, especially to those unaccustomed to it. It seemed to me as though the atmosphere was perspiring. I had expected to remain several weeks in this far-famed city, but on the second day I was all but exhausted, and hastily secured passage by the China merchant-steamer *Pautah*, Captain Lancaster, for Chefoo, to leave next morning at day-break. Once out of the river and on the open sea, the air grew cooler, and each inspiration seemed like a tonic. Ugh! the beastly climate of Shanghai in summer. All the residents who can do so leave in summer for Chefoo or Japan, and return after the rainy season is over.

The China Sea is nearly always choppy, and our voyage up to Chefoo was no exception to the usual rule; so we were very glad to end it by arriving on time, Friday, 9 A.M., June 26th. We anchored a half-mile from shore, and were immediately surrounded by numerous sampans, anxious to secure passengers desiring to go ashore. These were manned by the North Chinamen among whom I had come to live. What sturdy fellows they seemed! Larger framed and much darker skinned than the Cantonese or Shanghai natives. While debating how to hire a sampan I was introduced by the captain to a Mr. Seth, an Englishman in the Chinese Customs' service, who kindly invited us to go ashore in the Customs' launch, which was about to return to the shore. We gladly accepted this offer, for the Chefoo sampan is a very uninviting boat. The Japanese sampan is always shiningly clean. The Shanghai sampan is comparatively clean, and has a neat cover, giving it some appearance, at least, of shelter; but a Chefoo sampan is generally filthy, leaky, and uncomfortable. If they only had such an ocean pier at Yokohama and Chefoo as there is in Kobe, how much trouble, and also danger, would be saved the poor globe-trotter in his peregrinations!

Thanks to the Customs' boat, we were soon standing safely on the wharf and could take in the surroundings. These consisted in a range of mountains about three miles away, and a range of coolies (demanding the privilege of carrying our luggage) but three inches away, with a town in between, as we could occasionally see, over the coolies' heads. Miss Anderson, a fellow-passenger, soon dismissed the coolies by selecting a man for each valise, telling him where to take it, and how much she would pay him, with a fluency that surprised the coolies as much as it did me. Then she led us to the business-house of Messrs. Cornabe & Co., where we waited, rather impatiently, until sedan-chairs could be procured to carry my wife and Miss Anderson to the residence of Dr. Corbett, a distance of two miles or more from the settlement, to whom we bore letters of introduction. In a few moments four coolies arrived with two ordinary matting-chairs placed upon poles, carried by two men each. My wife rather tremulously took her seat in one, Miss Anderson assuring her it was perfectly safe; but when the men raised her from the ground, she could not suppress a little feminine scream and an appealing look toward me. " Oh, it's all right, my dear," I answered, in an assuring tone, though I confess I did feel quite nervous at the pace at which they moved off, without even a hand on the cross-bar that rested on their necks, depending on their equality of gait to prevent the chair dropping to the ground. But after proceeding a half-mile, seeing they were so sure-footed, I took courage, and became more interested in the scenes about me. I saw at a glance that the foreign portion of Chefoo, or the settlement as it is called by the English residents, was a very small place, and could no more be compared with Shanghai than a country village could with New York. Only a few stores, a few hotels, a few sailors' taverns, and three or four warehouses, with the consulates of the various nations doing business at this port, and that was all there was to see. Then, passing out of this locality, which is on a slender neck of land, we came to the native city of Chefoo, or, rather, Yent'ai, as it is known to the Chinese,—a city with a dilapidated wall on the west side,

Ruined Temple of the Tung Ta Tz's at Têng Chow Fu.

having a population of about thirty thousand souls. Through the streets of this city we passed without exciting any comment, but on every side of us arose such smells that I became sick at the stomach. Every man, woman, or child who passed was reeking with an odor which I took to be catarrh, but which proved to be due to a certain vegetable they are fond of eating, resembling a leek, and called chiu ts'ai. Then, too, every one's clothes were filthy, and naked children were playing right in our paths. Women sat in door-ways nursing children from bosoms covered with grimy dirt; men sat in the shade turning over the waists of their pantaloons looking for the inevitable gray-back louse. The sun shone down hot on the dusty path, and, perspiring from every pore, I arrived, disgusted, weary, and half-sick, at Dr. Corbett's bungalow. A bungalow is a one-story house built upon a foundation raised about three feet from the ground, and usually having a portico around two or more sides.

Residents in the East become so used to living in one-story houses that they find, on returning to their native lands, that two- or three- story houses are a nuisance not to be endured. Dr. Corbett's residence was situated half-way down what is known as Temple Hill, and, being elevated considerably above the town and harbor, commanded a beautiful view of both. There was a wide piazza on the front and east side the length of the house, which afforded a delightful promenade even in the rainy season. We were warmly welcomed by the good doctor and his wife, and comfortably installed in a suit of rooms consisting of a study, bed-room, and bath-room. Our baggage had arrived before us, and, though I had feared, from the apparently loose way in which one coolie had grabbed a valise and made off, another a parcel, and two or three more a trunk, and so on, that something at least would be stolen, I was agreeably disappointed on finding the packages all there, and all intact. We had only time for a bath and change of linen, when we were summoned to luncheon, and as we ate we discussed with our host and hostess our plans for the future. They assured us we might remain in Chefoo as their guests until autumn without in the least inconveniencing them, and that the doctor would procure a teacher for us and help start us in the language. Thus, deciding that we would not go into the interior until autumn, we settled down comfortably in Chefoo, with the intention of acquiring, as rapidly as possible, the language of North China, the kuan hua, or official language.

CHAPTER I.

THE Monday morning after our arrival I was called by Dr. Corbett, to be introduced to the gentleman who was to act as my teacher. I found in waiting a tall, pleasant-looking man, dressed in a long blue-cotton gown, with smoothly-shaven face and head and a shining, black queue of heavy, coarse hair, neatly plaited, reaching from the back of his head to his heels. He arose on my entrance, and, upon Dr. Corbett's stating that I was the pupil who required instruction, made me a profound bow, which I awkwardly endeavored to imitate. " This is your teacher, a Mr. T'an, from near Ching Chow Fu," said Dr. Corbett. " He does not understand a word of English, and is not a scholar of marked learning; but he is a clear speaker and an intelligent man, and I believe you will find him better at first than a more learned man, who would perhaps not be as patient." " But if he does not understand any English, how am I to ask him questions, or how understand his answers?" I ventured. " You will not need to at first. None of the teachers speak English, and yet we have all acquired the language. But first we must find you a name, for Mr. T'an has already inquired your name, and I have been obliged to inform him that as yet you have none." " What, am I not to be called Dr. Coltman?" I asked, surprised beyond measure, and not at all pleased at the idea of losing my identity, so to speak. " No; that is impossible," he replied, with an amused smile at my greenness. " You see," he continued, " the Chinese can

(13)

only pronounce words already existing in their language, and, besides, they have a hundred names which are called the hundred family names, and every foreigner upon arrival in China selects or has selected for him a name from the list of family names, which he is ever afterward known by. It is usual to select a name bearing as nearly as possible some resemblance to the English name formerly owned by the individual. Now, in your case I think the name Kou will be as near Coltman as we can get; but I will ask Mr. T'an, as his opinion is better than mine." Thereupon ensued a dialogue of a few minutes' duration, during which I could only catch the words Kou, man, and Coltman, repeated at intervals. At its conclusion Dr. Corbett turned to me and said, " Your teacher is of the opinion that Man is a better name for you than Kou, and if you like it you will be from henceforth Mr. Man, or, as they cannot say *Mister*, you will be known to the Chinese as Man Hsiensheng, and your name written out will be thus: 满先生 But you will need two characters in the place of your name of Robert, which is unpronounceable, as the Hsiensheng 先生 is used for all who are entitled to be called Mister, or teacher." Then another dialogue took place, which resulted in my being clothed (though hardly, in my right mind) with the name Man Lo Tao, written thus: 满乐道 After this important decision had been arrived at, the doctor produced a book of Chinese and English lessons, the first lesson of which is reproduced here, and said, " Your teacher will point to each character and pronounce the name of it, which you will repeat; when you pronounce it correctly he will go on to the next, and so on down to the end of the page. Then he will recommence at the top and repeat as before until you can remember and correctly pronounce them all." " Do I have to remember a page a day?" I asked, looking helplessly first at the page before me, and then at T'an Hsiensheng's smiling face, who seemed eager for the fray. " Oh, suit yourself. When you are tired, dismiss your teacher, who will wait outside in the teachers' quarters until you want him again. And now I will leave you alone, and wish you a pleasant morning's study."

The following page represents the lesson. I seated myself on one side of the table; Mr. T'an, or T'an Hsiensheng, as I shall now call him, bowed and sat down at my side. Then we looked at each other and smiled; then, pointing to the first character (an ordinary dash), he said " Ee." " Hum; that's easy," thought I; " anybody can say that." " Ee," I repeated. " Day la," he said, before passing on to the next. I mentally wondered what " day la " meant. Again he points, this time to No. 2, and says " Erhl." I looked at him and hesitated. He repeated it; " erh " or " erhl," I could not tell which. I endeavored to repeat it. Evidently I had not got it right, for he kept repeating it, and each time I answered he muttered, under his breath, " Bu day, Bu day." I had a suspicion he was invoking Buddha to help either he or I; but finally I must have caught the right tone, for, to my relief, he said " Day la " and passed on to the next.

My tongue never seemed so clumsy. Time after time I was obliged to repeat the same character before my patient teacher was satisfied with my pronunciation, and, after finally saying it correctly the first time, I was much mortified to find, the second time, I was as unable to pronounce it as before.

一	ee	one
二	erh	two
三	san	three
四	ssu	four
五	wu	five
六	liu	six
七	ch'i	seven
八	bah	eight
九	chiu	nine
十	shih	ten
百	bay	one hundred
千	ch'ien	thousand
兩	liang	two
人	ren	man
女	nü	woman
來	lai	to come
去	ch'ü	to go
出	ch'u	to go out
個	kŏ	numerative of many things.
回	hui	to return

For two hours I repeated, poll-parrot fashion, these queer-sounding names, till, worn out, I concluded to take a rest before proceeding farther. I leaned back in my chair and laid down my pencil, looking T'an Hsiensheng in the face, to see if possible, from his expression, what he thought of me. He gazed thoughtfully at the ceiling, then at the floor, and finally at me, when, seeing my puzzled expression, he smilingly made some pleasant remark. Then it dawned upon me that I was unable even to dismiss him politely; so, leaving him sitting alone, I made my way over to Dr. Corbett's study and requested him to come and tell the gentleman I was tired, and desired to rest. " That is unnecessary; you return and simply say ' Ch'ing,' and he will leave you. When you desire to study again, go to his door and say ' Ch'ing lai,' which is ' Please come,' and he will at once be at your service. How do you like him?" " I have no reason to dislike him, but he smells so horribly of garlic that the room seems pervaded with the odor." " It is hard to prevent them eating the garlic and chiu ts'ai, a kind of leek," said the doctor; " but I will speak to him and request him to abstain from it for awhile. After you have been here some time, you will not notice it." I returned, and, as directed, said " Ch'ing." Upon hearing this, T'an Hsiensheng bowed and walked out. Left alone in the study, I sat for some time gazing at the page I had been endeavoring to commit, wondering if I should ever be able to read these characters fluently, and suchlike musings. Then I turned over a page to lesson No. 2, and there, as I had expected, the characters were much more complex. " Sufficient unto the day is the evil thereof" came into my mind. " I will not worry over to-morrow's lesson until to-morrow."

Closing my book and donning the enormous pith-hat I had purchased in Shanghai, I raised a sun-umbrella and passed out the main gate for a ramble before luncheon. I walked directly eastward, down the hill, passing several small hovels, each with a garden-patch to the back, in which I observed onions, egg-plants, beets, and radishes growing in rows, with little gutters or trenches between, the moist condition of the trenches showing plainly that irrigation was relied upon to produce the crops rather than rain. A little farther on I was able to see the process by which these truck-gardens were irrigated. In one corner of the garden or patch was a well; a stone slab with a hole five inches in diameter stood on either side of the well. Through these holes passed a rough, round log, used as a windlass by means of an **L**-shaped handle attached to one end. A sturdy young fellow of about twenty drew up the water in a round basket holding about four gallons, and dumped it into an oblique stone trough in front of the well, by which it passed into the first trench, and from that into the others. This man wore neither hat, nor shirt, nor shoes; a pair of cotton trousers rolled up to the knees and tied at the waist by a piece of rope was his only clothing. With a thick pith-hat and a sun-umbrella I still felt the rays of the summer sun, but he, bare-headed and bare-backed, worked away as though trying to keep warm. His body was burned to the color of dark, undressed leather. Farther on I met another and much older man, whose naked shoulders and back were as black as an ordinary Virginia negro. After walking about a mile, I entered a small village of some thirty or more houses, mostly of adobe-brick, stone-faced. Not seeing any one about, I sat down on a stone under a tree to rest and look about me. A miserable, mangy specimen of the canine race soon caught sight of me from an adjacent door-way, and set up a howl or bark, which speedily brought all the dogs in the village to his assistance. I never saw a more mongrel collection of canines than was exhibited on this occasion. All looked three-quarters starved; some were blind; many had large, open sores on their bodies, and more than one was lame. By this time the villagers, hearing the turmoil, appeared in the door-ways, and I had become an object of interest to at least a hundred pair of eyes. Little naked boys stalked boldly out and ranged themselves in a semicircle in front of me, and, although I could not understand a word they said, I could see from their gestures they were alluding to the size of my pith-hat. The women and girls remained in their door-ways, where, collected in groups, they were evidently laughing at me. I felt very uncomfortable and got up to go, when an old man came out of the nearest door-way, and, nodding his head, asked me some questions. I could only shake my head, as I did not understand him, which seemed to amuse the small urchins very much. Bowing to the old gentleman, I hastily walked away, feeling that I must work hard and perseveringly at the language; for, to be unable to speak when spoken to made me appear a dummy, even to these simple villagers. Returning by the path I had come, I arrived in time for luncheon, or tiffin, consisting of broiled spring-chickens, green peas, potatoes, lettuce-salad, pickled beets, custard-pudding, and apricots.

I found, to my surprise, that the diet of the Americans in China does not differ materially from that at home; at least, in the port cities.

The Chinese are very apt in supplying any existing

want, and they no sooner find out what the foreigner likes to eat than they produce or import it. In Shanghai the market is as good as any and better than many cities of the world. Chefoo, Tientsin, and, in fact, all the port cities also, have very good markets. The mutton of China far surpasses that of the United States, and is said to resemble in taste the mutton of Scotland. Beef is usually obtainable, but, outside of Shanghai, is of inferior quality, as the animals are not fed for market, but are worked until old and then sold to the butcher. Veal is hard to obtain, as the natives object to killing the calves, which pay them much better as oxen or beeves. Chickens and eggs are produced abundantly, and are very cheap. Vegetables, such as spinach, cabbage, onions, sweet potatoes, celery, radishes, turnips, peas, string-beans, egg-plant, cucumbers, and squashes, are native to the soil; white potatoes, beet-root, and other vegetables introduced from abroad, thrive well. Several varieties of melons, peaches, apricots, plums, and grapes are native productions, but the fruit, with the exception of the apricots, cannot compare favorably with the American varieties. Walnuts, peanuts, and chestnuts are found everywhere, the latter resembling in size and taste the Italian chestnut. Strawberries, raspberries, and other berries have been introduced in the neighborhood of the port cities, and do well. Dairies have also been established wherever a community of foreigners exist; so that fresh milk and butter, those necessaries to every foreign table, are not wanting. Game in season is sold at very moderate prices, the feathered tribe of all varieties furnishing a contingent. Fish of a thousand shapes and sizes are sold for a mere song. Oysters, crabs, and lobsters for those who like them; and, with

Inside the Ch'ien Men Gate, Peking.

the merchant-houses furnishing foreign groceries, there is no luxury or necessary of the Western table that is not to be found in the ports of China.

My main business while in Chefoo, of course, was to acquire the language ; therefore, I studied each morning from breakfast-time until tiffin, reserving the afternoon for a siesta and a walk, and the evenings in making and receiving calls. Chefoo in summer is quite a lively place, considering its size.

All the boarding-houses, hotels, and even private residences are crowded with guests from the South, who, from fear of the heat or bad health, find Chefoo a pleasnt refuge. Visitors are coming and going ; vessels constantly arriving and departing ; excursion parties, nner parties, and picnics follow on each other so rapidly that much progress in the language is impossible. Students who go to Chefoo to spend the summer studying will depart in the autumn with pleasant recollections, but very little gained. At least, that was my case and the case of all those from the interior I met that first summer. The heat from nine o'clock until four or five was usually intense, but after five quite bearable and pleasant to either walk or ride. One day, on returning from a walk to the sea-shore west of the native city, I entered the city-gate to make a shorter cut for my quarters. Imagine my surprise, on glancing up as I emerged from the gate, to see three ghastly heads stuck upon poles just in front of me. The faces were all those of young men, and, to judge by their condition, had been recently placed there. A proclamation of some kind was attached to each pole, telling, doubtless, the crime for which the party had been executed. On my arrival home I asked my host if he knew anything of the occurrence. He said he had heard there had been stealing by the soldiers of the garrison in Chefoo, and insubordination, and that these men were probably soldiers. On investigation, this turned out to be the case. The men were proved to have stolen powder and sold it in the city, and on conviction were promptly beheaded as a warning to others. Another day I saw a man wearing a wooden collar four feet square and about three inches thick, called a caugue by the foreigners. A gentleman who was walking with me read the proclamation attached, which said the bearer was a liar and false witness. If all the liars wore wooden collars the forests of Korea would be insufficient to supply the necessary timber. As to the society one meets with in Chefoo, Shanghai, and the ports generally, I subscribe to the opinion of W. E. Griffis, in his excellent work on Japan. His opinion of Yokohama is my opinion of Chefoo. Being such a cosmopolitan place, the dweller in Chefoo must be always vigilant to offend none, and in all the windings of conversation must pick his steps, lest he tread on the national, religious, or æsthetic corns of his neighbors. What is complimentary to one man may be insult to some one else present, and so one becomes schooled to make only the correct remark. Though this state of armed neutrality may sometimes tend to make conversation excessively stupid, and a mere round of desiccated commonplaces, it trains one to be, outwardly at least, charitable to all, malicious to none. It keeps one circumspect and cosmopolitan, whether in opinions or moral practice; and to be cosmopolitan is to be, in Anglo-Oriental eyes, virtuous beyond vulgar conception.

The predominating culture, thought, manners, dress, and household economy in Chefoo, as in all Eastern

ports, is English. Outnumbering all the other nation-
alities; with their ever-present soldiers and navy; with
their unrivaled civil service, which furnishes so many
gentlemanly officials; and with most of the business
under their control, the prevalence of English thought and
methods is very easily accounted for. Because of the
very merits and excellences of the genuine Englishman,
the American in the East can easily forgive the intense
narrowness, the arrogant conceit, and, as relates to
American affairs, the ludicrous ignorance of so many
who arrogate to themselves all the insular perfections.
Perhaps most of the Englishmen in the East are fair
representatives of England's best fruits; but a grievously
large number, removed from the higher social pressure
which was above them, and which kept them at their
true level in England, find themselves without that
social pressure in the East and become offensively
vaporous in their pretensions. They are the foreigners
in the East who believe it is their duty to whip, beat,
cuff, and kick their servants upon the slightest occasion,
and show to all, by their treatment of their servants, how
little time has elapsed since they were servants themselves.
No one need take offense at this unless he feels guilty.

The residents of Chefoo all think it a most desirable
place in which to live, but many who go to spend a
summer only come away with a bad impression of it. It is
called a health resort; the Newport of North China, etc.
For a health resort it can show more fatal cases of diar-
rhœa, dysentery, and cholera than any city on the coast.
It is fast losing the reputation it once held. Doubtless the
proximity, I should say the continuity, of the native city,
with all its filth and disease-breeding slums, has had
considerable to do with this latter-day complaint of un-

healthfulness. Although some distance away and above the city, yet, whenever a wind blew from the north the air on our front piazza was malodorous to a painful degree.

Nearly two months passed in this daily routine of study and recreation, and then I could understand a simple sentence or two of Chinese. Among the first words I learned were "Chin lai," come in; "Kuan shang men," shut the door; "Ch'ing tso hsia," please sit down; and "Toa shao?" how much? I used to take T'an Hsiensheng with me on walks into the native city, where we would purchase a few peaches, apricots, or plums, he explaining as well as he could the various terms used in buying and selling. In this way I soon acquired a knowledge of sufficient words to enable me to make a purchase myself. I felt quite proud the first day I walked up to a peach-vender's stand and successfully negotiated for ten luscious peaches.

T'an Hsiensheng proved so willing and helpful as a teacher that I decided to take him along with me when I moved into the interior. His salary was the magnificent sum of five dollars per month and no extras. With this amount of money I was told he could feed and clothe himself very comfortably in native style. A native woman we employed as nurse to our little boy received three dollars per month, and supported herself and husband upon it. All the teachers, helpers, and servants connected with foreigners appeared extremely neat and cleanly; while those in the native city, without exception, were dirty, careless, and slovenly. A Chinaman can adapt himself to circumstances with great ease. Naturally dirty and careless, he will, when he finds it to his interest, become scrupulously clean; at least, to all outward appearance. If the interest ceases, he will speedily relapse into his former careless and dirty habits and attire. No doubt poverty has something to do with the filthy appearance of many of the natives; but it is not alone responsible, for I have met many men whose external garments were of rich new silk or satin, whose under-garments, once white, were now nearly black, having been worn an entire winter without change. If a man has but one garment we can excuse him for not washing and changing during the winter months; but where his means will allow of a change we cannot but condemn him as exceedingly filthy if he does not observe ordinary cleanliness of person and attire.

At first I could not distinguish a man from a woman, but in a little time I could tell, from the hobbling walk of the bound feet, a woman from a man at the distance of a mile. All wear the blue-cotton blouse and pants who are not able to wear silk; unless, indeed, they are in mourning, in which case they wear white. Red is the color betokening rejoicing, and is used at marriages; also for hangings and streamers on festive occasions. White is for mourning. Blue is the favorite color for general wear. Yellow is the imperial color, and in every city there is a temple, dedicated to the worship of the Emperor's tablet, whose walls, gates, sides, and roofs are all painted yellow. One morning, near the close of my stay in Chefoo, T'an Hsiensheng told me there would be a theatrical exhibition at the temple, just above us on the hill, and asked me if I would care to go up and witness the performance. I gladly consented; so, together we climbed the steep hill and soon stood on a little stone platform, some twenty odd paces from the front of the stage. A wooden platform, about twenty feet front by forty feet deep, had been erected upon stout

bamboo poles; coarse mats covered the top and three
sides, leaving the front facing the temple open. A screen
at the back served as a dressing-room, though, as it only
covered two-thirds of the space, we could frequently see
the actors changing their costumes. There was no
drop-curtain. On our arrival the play was already in
full blast; the drums were beating, a squeaky fiddle was
screeching, cymbals were clashing, and amidst the
horrible din a man dressed like a woman was singing at
the top of his voice, in falsetto, to an old gentleman
whose false, white beard of horse-tail kept blowing away
from his face, revealing a smooth-shaven chin. A crowd
of some five hundred men, women, and children stood
around, apparently enjoying the show as much as we in
Western lands would a performance of Booth or Irving.
Observing that I divided the attention with the per-
formers, I soon had enough and beat a hasty retreat.

A day or two following this I received from Chinanfu
a telegram stating that Mr. Bergen would go to Tientsin
and meet me in two weeks' time, to escort me to the
interior. This was only the third telegram over the
newly-completed telegraph-line established between
Shanghai and Peking, with a branch line from Chining
Chow to Chefoo. We thus had evidence that China
was making one move, at least, in the right direction, as
this was the first line established in the country. Having
received from the United States Consul at Chefoo my
passport to the interior, signed by Secretary of State
Bayard, bearing also the stamp of the Tsung li Yamen,
I considered myself invincible, for I was fortified with
the arsenals of Uncle Sam and the permission of the Son
of Heaven (as his Imperial Majesty is designated). So
we prepared to move onward.

CHAPTER II.

ON the morning of August 31st we were looking anxiously with glasses, from the piazza of the Corbett bungalow, at the signals displayed by the Customs' Signal-office, to see if there was a steamer coming from the South. Shortly after 9 o'clock a big black ball ascends to the yard-arm on the extreme right, and we are thereby informed that our vessel is sighted. We take a hasty farewell of the friends who have been so kind and hospitable; give the word to go to T'an Hsiensheng, who has command of the little army of coolies engaged to carry our trunks, valises, and boxes; take our seats in the sedan-chairs; and move at a lively pace down hill to the jetty, where we take the steamer. The steamer is just dropping anchor in harbor upon our arrival at the wharf, and we can see her some half a mile from the shore, already beginning to discharge cargo into the myriads of sampans that swarm about her. On application for passage at the office, we are told, "She is all full; every berth taken." "What are we to do?" Unsympathetic clerk replies, "Don't know." Of course, it is impossible to take a deck-passage with a wife and baby; and no other steamer was expected for several days. In the midst of this dilemma the captain of the steamer arrives, and, on learning that there is a gentleman with his wife and baby anxious to go by that steamer to Tientsin, gallantly offers his state-room. I am introduced to Captain Gregson, of the *Taku*, who presses me to accept his cabin, and, under the press of

(27)

circumstances, I gratefully yield. We are now all right.
Trunks, boxes, and valises, in company of T'an Hsiensheng, embark in sampans and make for the vessel's
side. We accept the invitation of Dr. Henderson, the
Customs' surgeon of the port, and are conveyed to the
steamer in his beautiful launch. It is late in the afternoon before the cargo is all taken in or put off and the
Taku steams out of Chefoo harbor. How refreshing to
be again upon the ocean! The odors of a Chinese city
no longer reach us; all is fresh and pure. Our fellow-
passengers are all Frenchmen: the French ambassador,
his secretary, the legation doctor, and three priests. These
fill the six wee state-rooms of the *Taku*, for she is a very
small steamer, and is built for the freight traffic rather
than to carry passengers.

The voyage is a short one. We reached the bar at
the mouth of the Pei Hŏ River in twenty-four hours
after starting. Unfortunately, the tide was low, and we
were obliged to remain outside the bar nearly twenty-
four hours before crossing. While we lay here waiting
I noticed the mate run up and down stairs from the
native steerage several times and hold a short interview
with the captain, who seemed uneasy at the information
received. Finally the captain came over to the side
where I was standing, and said: "Doctor, there is a man
among the steerage passengers very sick. Would you
kindly go and see what is the matter with him, as we
have no ship's doctor?" I gladly complied; and, upon
entering the crowded steerage, was led to a bunk in
which lay a man over fifty years of age. He was entirely
unconscious. His bed was saturated with the rice-water
stocls of Asiatic cholera, the floor and upper part of the
bed in the same condition from the vomited material.

His pulse was rapid, thready, and irregular; collapse complete, and death imminent. "What is the matter?" asked the mate, standing beside me. "Cholera," I replied. He did not wait for another word, but bolted up the companion-way, leaving me to follow more leisurely. The captain met me as I came up, and asked, "Is it genuine cholera, Doctor?" "Not the slightest doubt," I replied. "Then we shall be quarantined, I don't know how long, at Tientsin," said he, "unless, Doctor, you keep quiet about it." "If you land this man at once and no more cases occur in our passage up the river, I shall say nothing, as I am anxious to land myself," I said. The orders were given with a rapidity scarcely believable, and, by the time I had mixed a dose of paregoric and brandy and given it to the poor fellow, he was lifted, bed and all, into a boat, lowered to the water, and rowed hastily ashore, where, with a friend, he was left at an inn. Cholera was raging in the native quarters when we left Chefoo, and this man had come direct from the infected district. Carbolic acid was freely used; the deck, bunk, and, in fact, entire steerage were soon reeking with the smell of it, much to the disgust of the Chinese passengers, who little realized their own danger from contagion. Twenty-four hours later, when we left the steamer, there had no other case developed.

At last the water rose sufficiently, and we steamed slowly across the bar, grating in several places over the sandy bottom. Once into the river, we looked for a speedy passage up and the sight of the busy city of Tientsin. These hopes were doomed to disappointment. Our captain, though a very pleasant gentleman, was a very poor skipper. The river from Taku to Tientsin is full of sharp bends, and is very narrow also; so that its navigation requires more than ordinary skill. Thirteen times we were run into the bank, and sometimes so strongly as to require several hours' work to get us off. The night of the second day out of Chefoo found us stuck fast in the Pei Hŏ River, and in danger of being eaten by mosquitoes. They settled down on us in swarms. Sleep was impossible; the only relief was in sitting in the close cabin and smoking vigorously. The problem my wife had to face was how to keep the mosquitoes from carrying off the baby bodily. In spite of all our efforts, he looked in the morning as though he had broken out with small-pox. All on board welcomed the light of dawn. None had been able to sleep. By four o'clock in the afternoon we had proceeded to within seven miles of Tientsin; but, alas! our bow was four feet up on the left bank, and a rope tied to a tree on the opposite bank and to the stern of our boat, with which a donkey-engine was making extraordinary efforts to pull us off, proved unavailing. A Customs' launch passing by was signalled, and kindly consented to take the passengers to Tientsin. Instructing T'an Hsiensheng to stay aboard and watch our baggage, or to engage a sampan and escort it to the Globe Hotel, we took our seats in the launch and left the miserable little *Taku* to her fate.

An hour's ride in the launch, and we were landed on the bund of Tientsin, in front of the Custom-house. Here the usual number of coolies and jinrickshaw-men were awaiting jobs, and I had a chance to put my slender knowledge of Chinese to the test. Picking out a well-built rickshaw-man, I inquired, " Ni chih tao San Hsiensheng ti Chia ma ? " (Do you know where Mr. Stanley lives ?) "Shih wo chih tao," he replied. (Yes,

I know.) "Then, take us there," I said. And we took seats in the vehicles of this and another coolie, and were rapidly carried away from the bund. I was immensely pleased to think that I had been understood, and in my hurry had not bargained for the fare,—a very important omission.

After a run of six or eight minutes we arrived at the residence of Mr. C. A. Stanley, to whom I bore letters of introduction. He happened to be out, but his servant could speak a few words of English, and told us we were expected, and to be seated and await his arrival. Having deposited my wife and infant in the parlor, I returned to the gate to settle with the rickshaw-men; but my good luck had left me. I could not understand a word they said, nor they me, apparently. I offered them ten cents apiece, then fifteen, then twenty,—all to no purpose. They had come to the conclusion that I was a stranger, and, not having made a bargain, they were going to bleed me to the utmost. I would probably have gone on increasing my fare until even their cupidity was satisfied; but the servant, who had heard a great deal of talk, came out and said to me, in English, "Mister, you go in house; I makee all right." I was glad to escape the settlement in this way. I went into the parlor, and the servant paid them five cents apiece and dismissed them. From this experience I learned the lesson, never to ride in a rickshaw or other conveyance in China without first settling the rate of fare to destination.

Upon the arrival of our host we inquired if the gentleman who was to escort us to the interior had arrived, and were told that nothing had as yet been heard from him; but not to be alarmed at that, as the

country west was all heavily flooded, and he might not
be able to reach Tientsin for a week yet. A week
passed, and still no escort. During this time we visited
the few points of interest (and they are very few) in and
about Tientsin.

The foreign settlement of Tientsin is just below the
large native city of the same name, and on the west bank
of the Pei Hŏ. There are more foreigners resident here
than at Chefoo, and the streets are wide, well macadam-
ized, and shaded. There are several good hotels, three
or four large business firms, and a number of smaller
ones. The native city above is variously estimated to
contain from five hundred thousand to nine hundred
thousand inhabitants. Tientsin is the first large city
south of Peking, and is the port of entry for merchandise for the north and northwest of the country. The
narrow, tortuous river is constantly filled with junks,
steamers, sailing-vessels, and smaller craft. Sometimes
you have to wait half a day or longer for your chance to
move up or down stream. Miles of masts and rigging,
from the most primitive mat-sail bound with grass rope
of the native cat-boat to the bleached canvas with
manilla roping of Norwegian brigs, are always in sight,
in profusion and confusion, The river-front presents a
never-ending panorama of passing boats, and the amount
of Chinese and foreign profanity, mixed fights, and
broken boat-hooks is a caution! Boats are bumping
into each other all the time, but, owing to the almost
imperceptible motion, no damage is done.

Nearly two weeks passed, and our escort had not yet
arrived. My impatience grew so great that I could wait
no longer. I accepted the services of a Mr. King, of the
C. I. M., who agreed to escort us up the Grand Canal to

The best Conveyance of North China, the "Ta Chiao," or Mule Litter.

Ssu Nüeh Ssu, and engage conveyance for us from that point to Chinanfu, our destination.

To be sure, I felt somewhat apprehensive of the journey from Ssu Nüeh Ssu across the flooded district, with my very limited command of the language; but I knew that a lady in that city was expecting my attendance in her approaching confinement, and felt the necessity of pushing on at all hazards. Having decided to move on, the first thing necessary was to hire what is known as a house-boat. These boats vary from twenty-four to thirty-six feet in length and from six to eight feet in width. Each boat carries a mast and one sail; the sail is used when the wind is favorable, but usually the crew of three men pull the boat by means of a rope attached to the top of the mast. From the extreme front of the bow to about midway of the boat is a miniature deck, which is removable in sections, disclosing the hold, whose capacity is, perhaps, one ton of cargo. Then comes a covered room the entire width of the craft and about ten feet in length, in which the passenger must, during his stay, live, eat, and sleep. Back of this is the cook-pit, only three feet long and the width of the craft, —barely room enough to hold two or three charcoal-stoves, a pail of water, and a few necessaries. At night the cook suspends everything from the roof of the apartment and sleeps on the floor. Back of the cook-pit, and on a level with the deck in front, is a rear deck some four to six feet long, where the steersman sits and manipulates the rudder. Two boards of this rear deck are removable, and reveal the cooking-room of the crew,— a space four by six feet. Here they cook and store their provisions. At night the crew wrap up in blankets and sleep on the forward deck. As there is only one small sleeping-room on each boat, we had to engage one boat for Mr. King and one for myself. This we were fortunately able to do for the sum of thirty thousand small cash each (equal to fifteen dollars Mexican currency).

I had just completed the hire of the boats, when, on returning home, I found my wife conversing with Mr. P. D. Bergen. Our escort had arrived at last. The tale he told of the condition of the country and state of the roads, due to the flood, was sufficient to have daunted us from taking the inland journey at this season, were it not for the reason already given. So, good or bad, we must push on, and, being blessed with a cheerful, plucky wife, I did not much fear the consequences. That afternoon our escort made out a list of the provisions we should need, and sent his own cook, whom, to our great joy, he had brought along, to purchase charcoal and other supplies necessary for a ten days' cruise on the pacific waters of the Grand Canal. Owing to the thoughtful care of Mr. Bergen, what might have been a very disagreeable journey was made not only tolerable, but pleasant. Travelers in China will appreciate this better when I state that he advised a bountiful supply of insect-powder and a small-mesh mosquito-net. Mr. King, who had been very willing at great personal inconvenience to escort us to Ssu Nüeh Ssu, was relieved of the burden.

On the night of September 14th, after tea, we bade farewell to Messrs. Stanley and King and went aboard our small craft, in order to get an early start next morning. Our bedding we spread upon the raised platform which occupied half of the little cabin, and underneath which we stowed our trunks and baggage. The only furniture of the cabin was one three-legged stool and a board hinged to one side, which did duty as a table and could be lowered when not in use. I brought along a small rocking-chair for my wife, and, although neither the apartment nor the *menu* was as elegant as a Pacific mail-steamer, yet we lacked nothing essential, and enjoyed the novelty of this method of travel. After an hour or two listening to Mr. Bergen's graphic description of his journey down to Tientsin, as we sat in our little cabin, but dimly lighted by a candle stuck in the mouth of an empty claret-bottle, we retired to bed. But not to sleep. At first the noise along the bund, where we were tied to a pier, disturbed us; the constant calling-out of cake-sellers, rice-sellers, and water-melon venders rendered sleep impossible; but toward midnight, when these noises had subsided, we were disgusted to find big brown roaches running all over the bed, and not paying the slightest attention to their path. If it lay directly over our faces, over they went. The first one that passed over my wife's forehead produced a scream that made me sit bolt upright and brought an inquiring " What's the matter?" from Mr. Bergen's boat, just alongside. " Matter!" cried my wife; " why, a big, horrid bug ran right over my face." " Oh! I guess it's the roaches," said Bergen, coolly. " Just give them a dose of insect-powder, and they won't disturb you." I arose, hunted around among our various boxes, and after nearly an hour's search discovered the tin of insect-powder we had purchased during the day. I did not tell my wife how many of these disgusting vermin I saw during my search; but, spreading a liberal supply all over the bedding, especially thick around the sides, bottom, and top, lay calmly down as if I had settled them. And it did, too. For the rest of the trip we were not bothered by roaches or any other vermin, but I became so used to the fragrant (?) insect-powder that I feared I could not sleep without it when I again became an inhabitant of a civilized dwelling. This, however, did not prove the case.

In the morning we were awakened by the bumping of our boat against others and the cries and shouts of the boatmen, all anxious to secure the right of way in advance of others. Hastily dressing, I stepped out on the tiny deck in front, where the two boatmen who composed the crew were poling up the narrow passage left in the middle of the stream. The skipper, a gray-bearded old Chinaman, burned to the color of an Ethiopian, sat calmly at the stern, with the rudder in one hand and a long brass-mouthed pipe in the other. In less than two minutes I had been punched three times in the ribs by the back ends of the long poles the crew were using, and concluded to seek the seclusion which the cabin granted.

Taking down the front two boards, I could see just as well, and ran no risk of being injured. For two hours we passed through rows of junks two and three deep on either side of us, threading our way up stream. Mr. Bergen's boat followed closely behind us, and from time to time, as we turned one of the numerous bends of that serpentine river, I caught sight of T'an Hsiensheng's clean-shaven face from the back of the second craft. Mr. T'an was installed in the little cook-box of craft No. 2, while Wang Shih Fu, the cook, occupied the rear of our boat with his pans, pails, kettles, etc. Soon after sunrise the savory odor of frying steak greeted our nostrils and bade us anticipate a speedy breakfast. Just outside and above the long line of boats there was more room, and we then made swifter progress; besides, a favorable wind was blowing, and the poling ceased, the sail was raised, and we sped merrily along. Mr. Bergen's boat came alongside, and he stepped on board for breakfast.

It seemed wonderful to me that in that little cook-box behind, with scarcely room enough to turn around, we could obtain any cooked food at all; but Wang Shih Fu did not seem to be at all incommoded. With two little charcoal-stoves at his feet and one on the little deck at his back, he deftly manipulated things so that we always had a good meal, promptly on time. That morning for breakfast we had fried beefsteak and onions, fried potatoes, boiled eggs, hot coffee, fresh bread and butter, strawberry jam, and bananas. Novelty gave us all good appetites, and, amidst much jesting, we cleared the board of all set before us. The wind soon shifted so as to be of no service to us, the sail was lowered, and the two men who had but recently been crew now became the engine; that is, they furnished the motive power. Attaching a long rope to the top of the mast, which was about twenty-eight feet high, they each tied a short, flat stick to the shore end by two ropes, one of which went under the other over the shoulder, while the stick lay obliquely across the chest. By pressing firmly against the billet as they walked, they pulled the boat along much the same as oxen in a yoke, and with about the same speed.

The current, which was pretty strong, was against us, and our progress was a regular snail-pace. We frequently stepped ashore and walked for several miles when the sail was not raised. The country was more or less inundated in all directions, and houses of adobe-brick crumbled and fell before our very eyes. Once in awhile we would pass through a town of some size on higher ground, and at such places, as soon as we tied to the bank while the men rested, or while the cook went ashore to purchase supplies, we would be surrounded by men, boys, and old women, all anxious to obtain a sight of the foreign woman and foreign baby. Very few foreigners had been along this route, and the curiosity of the natives, many of whom had never seen a white lady or a white child, was very great. The people were, however, all respectful, and, beyond their anxiety to catch a sight of us, never otherwise annoyed or ill-treated us. At night the boatmen rested, the boat being tied to the bank in some village or by some village; for, sometimes a village lay on both banks, and, again, only upon one bank of the canal. Nine days passed pleasantly enough in this way, and on the afternoon of the tenth we arrived at the decayed city of Ssu Nüeh Ssu.

Here we were to commence our overland journey to Chinanfu, eighty miles, which would take us three days to accomplish under ordinary circumstances, and more likely at present five or six, owing to the flooded condition of the country. Wang Shih Fu and T'an Hsien-sheng were sent ashore to secure conveyances. They soon returned with two carts, a sedan-chair, and two donkeys. Our luggage filled the two carts; Mrs. Colt-man and the baby occupied the chair, eight coolies being engaged to carry it alternately in relays of four; Mr. Bergen and I mounted a donkey apiece. Oh, that beastly ass! He took a dislike to me before I left the boat, and, on my taking a seat on his back, jumped and plunged in such fashion as threatened my enforced dismounting. "Hold on to him, Doctor," sang out Bergen;

" he's all right." " Yes, I see there is nothing apparently wrong with him; in fact, I think he is feeling immense!" I managed to hold him somewhere near that district until word was given to go, when I brought my umbrella down with a whack over the top of his head and let him go. For seven miles he scarcely slackened his gait, and in less than an hour's time we had arrived (that is, Mr. Bergen and I) at the village of P'ang Chuang, the extreme western station of the A. B. C. Board of Foreign Missions. Here we were welcomed by the missionaries and given a good, comfortable bed-room to sleep in. My wife arrived a little after dark, an hour behind us, and, although left alone in a strange country, seeing no one but the chair-bearers, not knowing where they were taking her, and unable to speak more than a few words of the language, still she said she was only beginning to feel uneasy when they arrived at the Mission. We were told by the missionaries that to the city of Yü Chĕng the roads were fairly good, but from there on the whole country lay under water.

Hiring a more amiable donkey, we next morning proceeded on our way. This beast was a chronic stumbler. I had not gone above half a mile when I was pitched over his head. He quietly waited while I picked up myself and my bedding and, with Wang Shih Fu's assistance, remounted. Another half a mile, and again I bit the dust. Mr. Bergen offered to exchange, but I would not consent. Another half a mile, another ungraceful descent, and then I was convinced that donkey-riding was not good form, and that I knew when I had enough of a good thing. Mr. Bergen said he was tired also, and that in the city of P'ing Yuan, just ahead, we would try and hire a wheelbarrow. " Do you mean to say you would ride on a wheelbarrow?" I asked, incredulously. "Oh, yes," he replied; "they are more comfortable than a donkey, and, besides, it is more sociable; seated side by side, we can converse with ease." I was anxious to see this wonderful vehicle. We were now passing through a level farming country, which appeared, as usual, thickly inhabited. At an interval of about a mile we would pass through a village of adobe houses with straw or reed roofs. These villages were usually surrounded by a decrepit adobe wall, and some even had a gate-house and heavy wooden gate. Trees grew within these village enclosures, but the plain was entirely free from tree or shrub, every available inch of ground being taken up by the cultivation of cereals. The dreary look of all of these villages made me feel home-sick. Nothing but dirty, mud-dried brick houses falling to decay everywhere, with some remnants of the red-paper mottoes pasted up last New Year's time, faded and filthy, still sticking to the miserable, rotten door-ways. Ruin and decay stared one in the face all the time.

"This part of the country is looking well," said the ever-cheerful Mr. Bergen. "Is it?" I asked. "Wonder what the other part is looking like," I added, under my breath. "The people all have plenty to eat, drink, and wear throughout this section, and the missionaries at P'ang Chuang find the work very hopeful," he continued. "You ought to see this country in the spring, Doctor, when the wheat is knee-high and every spot between the villages is a bright green; it is beautiful!" "Oh, yes; it must be," I assented, but with such an evident sarcastic inflection that Mr. Bergen looked up at me in surprise, and asked, "You are greatly disappointed, are you not?" "I don't know whether it's disappointment or this donkey," I answered; "but I don't feel like going into raptures over a lot of dirty mud-houses and a country which appears to be given over entirely to raising beans." "You will feel better after dinner," he said, with a tone of conviction. "See, yonder is P'ing Yuan, and we will get a good dinner and a wheelbarrow, after which I promise your spirits will rise."

A few minutes later we rode through the gates of the ancient city of P'ing Yuan, a walled city of perhaps twenty thousand inhabitants, like most other interior cities, fast falling into decay. From the outside, looking at its massive brick walls and pretentious gate-house, you might imagine fine houses, gardens, churches, or temples of magnificence, and public buildings of superb architecture were within. If you did, you would feel as mean as the houses when you saw the inside. Mud-brick, mud-brick, mud-brick everywhere. Scarcely a building in the city but looks as though it might tumble down overnight. The inns as bad as the houses,—mud-brick structures, with stables in the front of the guest-rooms, and the whole court-yard reeking with filth. Mr. Bergen had instructed Wang Shih Fu to go on ahead and secure the best inn; so, I suppose, the one we were taken to was a regular "Astor House" in its way. I pity those who stopped at the second-class establishments. The inn-keeper had nothing we would eat, excepting eggs; but Wang Shih Fu, the ever-faithful, ever-willing *chef de cuisine*, managed, from some unknown quarter, to produce fried chickens, cold ham, cold tongue, buttered toast, spinach, and eggs, with raspberry jam and a cup of tea.

A Chinese cook is a magician. Only let him know

for how many people he has to provide, and he will have a meal where it seems impossible,—provided he is in a good humor and can have his own way. Try to make him follow your plans as against his ideas, and you are sure to suffer from it. After dinner the cook spent most of the afternoon in securing a wheelbarrow, and finally succeeded in hiring one which agreed to take Mr. Bergen and myself as passengers to Chinanfu for twenty-five cents per day. It was too late to go any farther that day; so we quietly sat in the inn, chatting, until time to retire.

The next morning we were off bright and early: Mr. Bergen and I on the wheelbarrow, my wife in the sedan-chair, and Messrs. T an and Wang on the donkeys. The wheelbarrow proved much better than the donkey. This style of barrow is very different from that of American construction. The wheel, which is nearly four feet in diameter, is in the centre; on each side of the hub is a seat, upon which, when your bedding is placed upon it, you can either sit up or recline. A man in front grasps two handles, and has a strap pass over his chest to pull; a man behind, in similar harness, pushes. A mat stretched over a bamboo frame shields from the sun, and renders the heat endurable.

At noon we stopped an hour in the village of Li Chia Chai for lunch, and by night-fall reached the walled city of Yü Chĕng. As we passed through the gate of this city I heard some one yell out, " Foreign devils have come! Foreign devils have come!" And immediately a great rush commenced from all quarters, to get a sight of us. All the crowds we had met before were orderly and quiet compared to this one. On our entering the inn-yard selected for us by the cook, we were so jammed by the people that it was next to impossible to proceed from the wheelbarrow to the door. Mr. Bergen on one side and I on the other escorted my wife from her chair to the door of the room we were to occupy, and, once in, closed the door. In an instant the paper windows were all torn out, and hundreds of faces were peering in at us, like people looking at animals at the "Zoo."

Mr. Bergen went to the door and addressed the people, asking them, for decency's sake, to conduct themselves more quietly; but they only laughed at and jeered him. He then appealed to the landlord to put them out of the court-yard, but that individual declared himself powerless. My wife hung up a sheet inside of the window, but they reached through and tore it down, laughing at and jeering us all the time. For three hours we endured this persecution, and then it was so late that they left us and went away with the expressed intention of coming back in the morning to "see us off." Wang Shih Fu wanted to get us supper, but we told him to get a pot of tea and then make arrangements to get us away from that vile inn before day-break.

While we were discussing some bread and butter and tea Wang Shih Fu was scouring the town for information, and came back saying there was water from two to four feet deep covering the entire country from Yü Chĕng to Yan Chĕng, and that it would take an entire day's journey poled on a flat-boat to cross it. "Have you secured a boat?" asked Mr. Bergen. "There is none to be had," said the cook, greatly to my dismay. "Oh, yes there is," said Mr. Bergen. "You just hunt the city over; leave no spot unsearched; one thing is certain, we must leave here to-morrow by day-break, and you must find the means."

The cook smiled a bland smile and departed. After midnight he returned saying he had hired a boat and four men at an extortionate sum to start at day-break. None of us did more than doze, for fear of oversleeping ourselves, and by first break of dawn were up and dressed. Wang Shih Fu had settled our bill at the inn, and now led the way quietly down the street to the South Gate, through which we must leave the city. Just outside lay the boat, and we were about half-way to it undiscovered when some wretch of a boy espied us and yelled out, "Come, come, quick! The foreign devils are stealing away." Then people came pouring out of houses from all directions, and soon we were almost surrounded. Grasping my stout cane firmly, I struck out vigorously right and left, speedily causing those in front of the sedan-chair to give way, and in a few moments it was set down upon the flat-boat. All hands quickly scrambled aboard the boat, pushed off, and, amidst a yell and jeer from the hospitable people of Yü Chĕng, we left their city behind.

All day long we poled over what had a few months before been farming country, but now was a watery waste. In places we could see, by the trees and ruins, the remains of villages partially submerged. Where part of a village had been on higher ground, it still remained above water and made a little island packed with people, and with the crops of the whole village placed on the housetops. Sometimes the water became so shallow that all the men and chair-coolies had to disembark and help push the boat through the mud. This day seemed interminably long; but all things have an end, and so did that piece of flooded country. Near dark we reached the higher ground skirting the town of Yan

Chĕng, and, paying our boat's crew a handsome bonus
for the faithful manner in which they had served us, we
took seats upon the wheelbarrow and were, in an hour's
time, seated at the best of the miserable inns of Yan
Chĕng, awaiting one of Wang Shih Fu's suppers. As
we had arrived after dark, few people saw us, and so we
were free from the uncomfortable experiences of the pre-
ceding night. We were tired out with the heat and
slowness of the flat-boat trip, and, after a light supper,
betook ourselves to rest.

Sunday morning, the 27th of September, and last
day of our journey, dawned cloudy and windy. Although
it looked very like rain, we decided to push on, for we
were only twenty miles from Chinanfu, and all were very
anxious to arrive there. Promising our wheelbarrow-
men and the chair-coolies additional money if they
arrived early in. the afternoon, we had the pleasure of
seeing them quicken their ordinary pace until we were
actually making fair speed. Shortly before noon we
reached the Yellow River, known to school-rooms in
America as the Hoang Ho.

It was a very swift-running stream, one glance at
which was sufficient to account for its name. We embarked on a flat ferry-boat, in company with a troop of
Chinese soldiers, who regarded us with great curiosity.
Their captain and Mr. Bergen engaged in conversation,
none of which I could understand; but Mr. Bergen informed me that our destination and object in coming
were the subjects of inquiry. When told that I was a
physician, the captain wanted to have several of his men
treated; but Mr. Bergen assured him I had no medicines
with me, and that they could be examined and treated
by us on their arrival at the capital, at our public dis-

pensary.   The wind had been increasing steadily all the
morning, and, by the time we landed on the south side
of the river, was blowing a regular gale.   In consequence, the dust from the river-bank was blown in im-
penetrable clouds all over us, filling our eyes, nostrils,
and hair, and in a very short space of time rendering us
unrecognizable to our best friends.   There was no inn
we could stop at nearer than the city, and so we were
perforce obliged to continue our journey amidst this
blinding storm.   This last experience was certainly the
worst of our trip from any time since leaving America;
but at last, after four hours of blinding, stinging, alkaline
dust, we entered the West Gate of the city of Chinanfu,
and, turning sharply to the left, skirted the south wall
for a distance of a mile, and brought up in front of Mr.
Bergen's gate.

Mrs. Bergen was rejoiced to see her husband safe
again, as she had not heard from him for nearly a month,
twenty-six days being the time consumed by his trip to
and from Tientsin.   She even forgave us, the cause of
his absence, and, with all the heartiness of an Irish-
American welcome, soon made us feel at home in this
interior city, far from our native land, beyond the limits
of Western civilization.

City Wall of Têng Chow Fu, from the East.

CHAPTER III.

CHINANFU, sometimes written Tsinanfu, or even Tsi Nan, is a large city, and so typical of the class of interior cities as yet little affected by foreign intercourse, that a description of it will convey to the reader the condition of China before the ingress of the foreigner causes a change. For, just as certain as foreigners are allowed to enter the interior cities and compete with the natives in trade, the appearance of the city, as well as the manner of doing business, will alter to a considerable degree. The city proper is irregularly round in shape, surrounded by a wall thirty feet high, twelve to fifteen feet wide at the top. This wall is pierced by three gates,—the south, west, and east. The whole northern part of the city is occupied by a large pond, or fresh-water lake, and so there is no northern gate. These gates are massive archways about twenty-eight feet wide, surmounted by a temple-like structure, in which an idol of some sort has his residence, but is not visited to be worshiped. What his particular business is I cannot say; doubtless, to protect the city in some way. As all entrance to or exit from the city must be by these three narrow gates, and a large percentage of the day population reside in the suburbs without the walls, the passage through one of the gates from 6 A.M. until noon is a matter requiring time and patience. From noon until 4 P.M. they can be passed with facility, but from that time until night-fall they are again crowded. Carts, horsemen, wheelbarrows, burden-bearers, and pedestrians all mix, in one of these

(47)

gate-ways, in almost inextricable confusion. Every one is shouting to "make room," or "give way," the wheel-barrows are squeaking in a piercingly high treble, the heavy carts are rumbling over the uneven stone paving, and you would imagine this to be the most noisy *mélange* possible. You are mistaken. Let a cart break down, which is an accident of frequent occurrence, and you have confusion worse confounded. Now, I admit that you could not increase the "ran nao" (noisy wrangling); no, not by adding a second broken cart.

One of the first things civilization will do for these interior cities will be the abolishment of the narrow gates. The loss of time incurred by this ancient style of city-construction cannot be estimated. From the West Gate, passing directly across the city to the Kuan Ti Miao, a temple at the foot of the East Wall, is the great street. This street is wider and better paved than is usual in a Chinese city, and the shops which line its sides are pretentious and thrifty. There is no sidewalk on this or any other street. Pedestrian and equestrian use in common the twelve feet between houses. Two carts may pass on this street, but there are many in the city where the passage of two carts is an impossibility. The houses are all one-story high, and for the most part built of stone or brick, with tile roofs. The central and southern part of the city is the most aristocratic, occupying the higher ground. From the great street going north the ground gradually slopes down, until finally it ends in the lake.

This lake within a city-wall is quite a novel feature of the city. It is formed by the numerous springs of fresh water in the vicinity, and has a depth of about six feet on the average. It covers, perhaps, a square mile in extent, and serves as a breeding-pond for vast numbers of carp and other varieties of pond-fish. On its surface you may, of a summer day, see many fancily painted and fantastically carved boats, each conveying a party of silk-robed pleasure-seekers to one of the several island-temples which dot its mirror-like expanse. These temples in the lake are kept in repair by the wealthy people of the city, who use them as picnic grounds. Although there are idols in their limits, they are more for ornament than worship, and about the only visitors are the pleasure-seekers, who carry their repast and their wine, and visit the temples to carouse. Throughout the city every square contains at least one shop bearing the inscription, " Best opium sold here! " or, " Opium in small quantities for sale! " and the odor of the burning drug meets your olfactories from every quarter. This is a rich city, full of mandarins and their retainers, and consequently the opium vice is excessively indulged in. Prostitution, too, is very largely increased in all capital cities, and Chinanfu is no exception,—several streets in the northern part of the city, near the lake, being given up to brothels.

Now, what are the wares we see exposed for sale on the great street? Suppose we start from the West Gate and move eastward. Just inside the gate, on the south side of the street, we see the guard-house, a rickety-looking structure with a dilapidated wooden front. Here are stationed a half-dozen policemen, whose ostensible duty is to keep order within the gates, to close them at night and open them in the morning, but in reality their time is principally employed in smoking opium and gambling. Beyond this guard-house is the first shop, a rather small affair, devoted to

4

the sale of ready-made clothing. Evidently, this shop is patronized by only the poorer class, as the trousers hanging by the door are only blue cotton, of various shades. Across the street is a similar establishment. The second shop is what is known as a food-shop; very handy to the hungry traveler just entering the gates. This is not, however, a swell restaurant, such as may be found at the foot of Fu Rung Chieh Street, but only a small shop, selling dry bread, doughnuts, seed-cakes, and millet-gruel. No meats nor side-dishes are obtainable here. Opposite is a " cha huo pu," or junk-shop, where you may obtain anything, from a piece of thread to an iron anchor, and all at the lowest prices,—so says the sign.

The fronts of all these shops are taken down each morning and replaced at night. By this means the store is lighted and the whole inside rendered visible from the street. They average fifteen feet in depth by about twenty-one feet front. Back of the store there are usually other rooms, used as store-rooms, from which the front room is refurnished as sales make necessary. Next comes a tea-store,—not unlike our home tea-stores in appearance. Numerous large tin boxes contain the fragrant leaves, each having mystic hieroglyphics on the outside, by which that particular kind is known. Many people in the United States suppose that good tea can be bought in China very cheaply. This may be the case in the tea-producing regions, but is not so in Shantung. Good drinking-tea cannot be bought in Chinanfu for less than one dollar per pound. The sales of the tea-shop are more by ounces than pounds, however, for I notice that most of the purchasers come out with very small packages. Passing the tea-shop, we stand in front of a cakeshop. Here are displayed rows of greasy-looking cakes, which, from a Western point of view, are far from appetizing, but to the Oriental represent the height of the culinary skill. "Tien hsin" they call all these little cakes, as well as all manner of dessert, which means "point of the heart," or a free translation might mean "goes-right-to-the-spot goodies." These Chinese confectionery-shops suffer greatly by comparison with those seen in Japan. I never passed a Japanese confectionery without being tempted to purchase some of the wares displayed. The difference I found to be, that the Japanese wares seldom tasted as good as they looked, while the Chinese always tasted better than their appearance seemed to promise. We leave the tien-hsin shop behind, and are confronted by a sign reading, "Nei tsao p'i hsiang," which, interpreted, is: "Inside we make skin-trunks." If they make them inside they don't keep them there, for the narrow street is made narrower by the row of red-painted trunks placed in front of the store. Each trunk has a brass hasp and lock, which looks awfully substantial, but which comes apart on the slightest provocation. These trunks are more used for storing clothing in at home than for use in traveling, and every bride of any degree of respectability receives one or more skin-trunks as a wedding-present. They are all oblong in shape, and white, red, or tan-color outside, lined with blue cotton inside.

Next door to the trunk-store is a "cash-shop," or "exchange-shop," or "ch'ien p'u tzu," as the natives call it. A few feet back from the front of the shop is a high counter surmounted by a smooth stone slab, upon which is a pair of balances for weighing silver. Back of this counter stand several slick-looking young men, ready to

assure you that the piece of silver you have brought to
exchange for the copper coins called cash is of poor
quality, contains lead, and is of lighter weight than you
assert. They weigh it upon the scales before your eyes
and prove it light, produce a brilliant piece of pure silver,
and, comparing it with yours, prove yours an alloy; and
finally effect an exchange greatly below par, leaving you
several thousand cash worse off than you thought you
were. If you desire to *buy* silver they weigh it on
another scale. Now the dark color does not indicate an
alloy, it is only dirt which rubs off readily; and as the
cash you have brought to purchase with contain many
counterfeit and small, worthless coins, you will have to
pay an additional premium, for this extra-fine piece of silver, of sixty cash per ounce above par. Such is the difference between buying and selling. Unfortunately, the
copper cash is the only coin circulating in the interior.
Silver coins such as the Mexican dollar and the Japanese
fractional silver coins circulate in the port cities, but are
of no use in the interior. Silver in bullion, in the shape
of shoes weighing fifty ounces each of purest silver, is the
standard of value. Silver is exchangeable, in every city
or town of size, at about fourteen hundred cash per ounce.
The actual rate is always changing, and is never the same
in any two places. It depends to considerable extent upon
the amount placed on the market. These cash-shops
issue bank-notes good only in the city of issue, and in
reality good only at the shops issuing them, where they
are redeemable in copper cash. The notes are usually
in denomination of one, two, five, and ten thousand cash
each. Should a bank fail, which is a common occurrence, the holder of its notes is a total loser and has no
redress. Occasionally a broken bank will compromise

and resume business, but, as a rule, when its doors are closed, that ends its career. The bank-president, or head, if caught, will spend the remainder of his days in prison.

Beyond the cash-shop is another clothing-store, but this is a big place, the front of which only serves as an entrance to the mammoth establishment within. We step through the front room, back a dozen paces through a passage-way or court, and are ushered into a large room, whose sides are lined with shelves well filled with rich clothing. The polite proprietor bows and begs us to be seated; one junior clerk pours tea for us, while another offers the famous water-pipe. We ask to be shown some winter clothing. What colored silk and what fur do we esteem? asks a clerk. No matter, we reply; let us see all before deciding. Whereupon we are shown garment after garment of many-colored silks, of all degrees of fineness, and furs of great value. To be sure, he has cheap sheep-skin garments, which we see in a pile in one corner, but he imagines the "foreign teacher" wishes nothing but the best; so nothing he offers us is at a less figure than thirty taels (ounces) silver; equal in this place to forty-five Mexican dollars. And some of the garments are as high as seventy-five taels silver. After viewing clothes until wearied by their very profusion and richness, we thank the polite proprietor and, assuring him that we shall patronize him in the near future, resume our way down the street. A candle-shop is first passed, then a brass-worker's, next a shoe-store, followed in turn by a hat-store, a cloth-store, and a fresh-vegetable store, and we have come to the end of the first block. Passing a narrow cross-street, we continue our walk eastward down the great street. It gradually becomes wider as we proceed, and the shops are larger and more important.

Every little while we see some article displayed for sale of undoubtedly foreign origin, as a glass lamp, a hand-mirror, a tin basin, or an eight-day clock. Even though we are eleven days' hard journeying away from the coast, still we see some of the unmistakable products of Yankee genius. For instance, it gives one quite a thrill of pleasure to see a little clock with " Seth Thomas " marked on the face of it in good English letters, away off in the interior, perhaps in a city no white man ever set foot in before. We notice in one place a photographer's sign, with specimens of his skill displayed. If they were fair samples, I wonder he received any patronage. Any amateur with two weeks' practice could have done better, and his price is a dollar a copy, cabinet size.

About half-way across the city the street is the widest, and here in the early morning the market is held. As soon as the city-gates are opened in the morning, farmers and vegetable-sellers enter in great numbers, each with his two baskets of produce slung on either end of a pole carried on his shoulder, eager to be first to the great street to sell to the crowd, who at that time repair there to buy. This is only the vegetable, fruit, and fish market. The fuel-markets are in the yards of several of the large temples. The grain-market is in the west suburb, sweet-potato market the same. Each article of produce is sold at a particular place, doubtless ordained so by the founders of the city hundreds of years ago and never changed. At the commencement of the vegetable-market is a street running north and south, bisecting the great street into nearly two equal halves. The northern

portion of this street, after passing through a large orna-
mental arch, ends, or rather bifurcates, into two smaller
streets, one passing east and the other west of the Governor's yamen, which lies between them. This yamen is
the residence and business-office of the Governor, his secretaries, and hundreds of retainers. The buildings are
better than the ordinary yamen buildings to be met with
in a hsien city but, for the residence of a governor of
such a province as Shantung, appear poor and in bad
repair.

They are brick, one-story, tiled-roof buildings, as are
the majority of the houses of the city, and were they kept
in repair would answer well enough to lodge troops or
cattle in; but a governor! Well, if I were governor of
Shantung I would build a new residence. The yamens
of the Fan T'ai and Nieh T'ai, the provincial treasurer
and supreme judge, respectively, are of the same inferior
style of construction and in the same state of decay.
Two blocks east of the Governor's yamen, on the great
street, is the prefectural yamen wherein Mei Ta Ren, a
mandarin of the third rank, and a foreign hater of the
first rank, holds the fort. This gentleman has been a
prefect, in office, for over ten years, and wherever he
has held office has made it warm for the foreigners
within his jurisdiction. From the prefectural yamen
eastward to the great wall of the city the street becomes
narrower and the shops more mean, until at the last street
they degenerate into a barber-shop and a hot-water shop,
respectively, on the northwest and southwest corners of
the Li Shan Ting. While the great street, or "Ta
Chieh," as it is called, is the principal street, there are
many others filled with shops doing a thriving business.
Just inside the South Gate is a street devoted exclusively

to the coffin industry.   Here coffins of any cost may be procured, from a dollar to three hundred dollars.

Every Chinaman who is able to do so buys his own coffin during his life-time, of such size, material, varnishing, etc., as suits his fancy.   Should he become impecunious afterward he may pawn his coffin, but he will likely part with almost everything else first.   The thicker the wood composing the sides, bottom, and top, the better the coffin, and the more expensive.   The buyer's idea is to have a thick one, well varnished, so that the body may the longer resist decay.   Indeed, they often assert that if the coffin is heavy enough the body will never decay.   Throughout the city there are arches of stone called "p'ai fangs," erected by the relatives of some deceased worthy, to commemorate some real or fancied virtues of Dives, for it is only the rich who have these memorials after them.   I notice that these "p'ai fangs" all seem quite old, none that I have seen having been erected in the life-time of the present emperor.

I believe the custom of erecting this kind of monument will soon be a thing of the past.   Some of them are quite artistically carved with griffins, lions, and serpents; others are very plain, with carved inscriptions only. On the opposite page is a memorial arch erected to the memory of a Mrs. Sung, a widow of much wealth and great virtues.   The inscription in the large characters says: "She rejoiced in virtue and loved to bestow alms." If she did, ten chances to one it was with the idea of having this stone arch erected after her decease.   I have heard that in some cases these arches, like the coffins, were bought by the parties themselves prior to their decease.   Just under the arch of the city-gate are several

The Sung Family Memorial Arch, outside the East Gate of Têng Chow Fu.

small boxes which look like chicken-coops. These are receptacles for the shoes of ex-magistrates of the city. Whenever a magistrate ingratiates himself into the hearts of the people, they request his shoes on his leaving for another post, and place them in a cage in the gate-way by which he leaves the city, to remain until they decay. Outside the city proper is what is known as the suburb, being really a continuation of the city, having its business streets and residence streets the same as in the city. The suburb is surrounded by a stout stone wall some fifteen or eighteen feet high, pierced by seven or eight gates. Many people doing business or employed in the city reside in the suburb, rents being much cheaper in the latter.

Owing to the overflow of the Yellow River and destruction of property and land in the vicinity of Chinanfu, the city has become the refuge of thousands of homeless wanderers, and their condition is pitiable in the extreme. There is not sufficient work to give them employment, and so they beg from door to door in hopes of obtaining sufficient nourishment to sustain life. Thirty thousand people were fed one good meal of millet daily from the kitchens established by the Governor and wealthy citizens during a period of three months the first winter. Afterward, either from deaths or removals, the number became greatly less each year, but even to-day there are a number of thousands dependent upon public assistance. These unfortunate people are not like the professional beggar, who never has worked and never will work. They were once thriving farmers, but the Yellow River flooding their lands for three or four successive years has deposited several feet of sand over the soil and rendered it useless; the glut of the labor market renders employment unobtainable, and nothing is left to them but to emigrate or remain and beg until they starve.

The Chinese cannot well find fault with the United States for forbidding pauper immigration when their own governors practice the same policy. The Governor of Shan hsi found his province was becoming fast peopled with the pauper refugees from Shantung and forbade their coming. He also remonstrated with the Governor of Shantung to such effect that the latter gentleman issued a proclamation forbidding his people to leave the province, under severe penalties if they disobeyed. There are no such institutions as public workhouses or public poor-houses. The rich contribute in times of great calamity very generously, but the government is not such as to apply the aid to the best advantage. The Emperor grants from the royal treasury immense sums at a time, to alleviate the misery of his people, but after the money or grain has passed through numerous hands to reach the people it is very much less than at first.

The shop-keepers of Chinanfu must find it very burdensome to be continually tossing a cash to the beggars. A beggar stands in front of nearly every shop in the city. He or she remains until a cash is tossed out. Sometimes it is a quiet beggar, who simply stands in front, with his tattered clothing and pinched face, silently waiting the cash which, sooner or later, will be given him. Sometimes it is the vociferous beggar, who howls and moans until he obtains his coin. Again, it is the musical beggar, who walks up to the counter and rings a cow-bell, without intermission, until he is bought off. The poor shop-keeper has no relief from this nuisance.

As soon as one moves on another takes his place, and thus it continues all day long and day after day. They never expect more than a cash at a time, equal to one-tenth of a cent, but even at this small figure the shop-keepers find them a terrible bore. Sometimes they are covered with frightful sores from head to foot; sometimes they are lepers; frequently they are blind. The blind beggar excites more sympathy than any other, and his cash receipts are consequently in excess of the other unfortunates.

Chinanfu is variously estimated to have from two hundred thousand to five hundred thousand population. Perhaps three hundred thousand would be a fair estimate. Being the capital of the province, there are more officials in it than in any other city of Shantung, and in its streets the silk dress of the mandarin is in striking contrast to the numerous beggars all about. Rich furs and heavy silks constantly jostle against tattered blue cotton, as the haughty ruler passes the cringing beggar, or his but little better off compatriot, the coolie. In the west suburb there are a great number of Chinese Mohammedans, who worship in two mosques inscribed with the Arabic characters. Only the priests can read them. These Mohammedans are much disliked by the other Chinese of the city, who consider them the descendants of outsiders. They are, however, but the descendants of converts to Mohammedanism, introduced into the country, the same as Buddhism, through India. These Mohammedans abstain from the flesh of swine, and are the beef-eaters of China. An ordinary Chinaman prefers pork to beef or any other meat; the Mohammedan esteems beef the best. There are many military mandarins who belong to the Mohammedan religion, some of whom have quite ancient family-records and considerable wealth.

In the southwest suburb there is a temple enclosure, within which is a wonderful spring bubbling up from the centre of a small pond. This spring furnishes an immense volume of water, supplying all the residents of that quarter and filling the city-moat. Many years ago it had a wonderful reputation as a curative agent, and pilgrims came from afar to visit it and drink its waters. A fair was established in consequence, in order that those visiting the spring might combine business with a desire to improve their health. The fair still survives. Every year, in the third moon, for a period of twenty-eight days, there is an immense concourse of people at the "Pao T'ou Ch'uan," as this spring is called. Booths are erected, jugglers perform feats of magic, sweetmeats are sold in all colors, flowers, pictures, crockery, tinware, brass-ware, and jewelry all are on exhibition, and a thriving trade is done.

The city proper is always filled with strangers during the progress of this fair, and the women and girls are allowed the unusual privilege of riding uncovered, on wheelbarrows or sedan-chairs, through the streets of booths. Certain kinds of baskets and other wares can only be purchased at this time, and many of the housewives depend on the fair for a year's supply of these goods. Numerous pilgrims to the far-famed T'ai Shan Mountain, with their unshaven heads and pilgrim staffs, break their journey at the fair, on their way to or from the devotional mountain, and add to the mixture of assembled humanity a flavor of religious element otherwise lacking.

CHAPTER IV.

In January, 1886, the first opportunity offered of paying a visit to the country people. Rev. Mr. Bergen, being obliged by duties pertaining to his work to make a country trip, invited me to go along. Although six months in the country, my available stock of language was still far too small to have ventured alone; therefore I gladly accepted this offer, and made preparations for a brief trip to the northeast of the city of Chinanfu. My friend advised me to discard prejudice and adopt the native dress, as he had done, assuring me that I would find it more comfortable in the biting cold, and that I would be less bothered by oft-repeated questions about the make-up and materials of my clothes, as well as less subjected to abusive language. To all of this good advice I turned a deaf ear. I was imbued with the idea that it was foolishness to change American clothes for Chinese; to discard the dress of civilization for that of heathendom. So I somewhat curtly informed him that he might become a Chinaman if he desired, but that if I could not go dressed as a decent citizen of the United States I would stay at home until able to go alone. His good nature was proof against this sarcastic speech, and he assured me I might dress in any way I preferred, his only concern being my comfort. Many times the next week I regretted my stubbornness and wished for a good, warm, sheep-skin " p'i ao," such as my reverend friend wore. Warned that it would be very cold, as all our route lay along the bank of the Yellow River, I tried to

(61)

dress so as to keep out the cold.   Next my body I wore
a warm suit of flannel; then a blue-flannel shirt, two
pairs of woolen pants, two vests, a stout woolen coat, a
heavy overcoat, a soft-felt hat, and pair of mittens, with
heavy button-gaiters, completed my attire.   We were to
go on a wheelbarrow to the city of Chi Yang, on the
north bank of the Yellow River, and from there to the
village of An Chia Miao, some fifteen miles farther east.
I packed a box with some medicines, a pocket-case of
instruments, and my dental forceps, as Mr. Bergen
assured me the natives would greatly respect me if I
could relieve some of their sick.

We decided to walk until outside the suburb gates,
as the barrow could make better progress through the
crowded streets if not loaded, besides saving us much
jolting over the uneven stone pavements.   We sent
the barrow on ahead, after first loading on it our necessary bedding, while we finished a hearty breakfast.   At
nine o'clock we "ch'i shen," or, as the interpretation is,
"moved our bodies" out of the gate of Mr. Bergen's
comfortable home, and, facing a strong north wind,
started on our journey.   Mr. Bergen looked a veritable
Chinaman,—Chinese hat, Chinese queue (sewed in the
hat), Chinese sheep-skin long-garment, Chinese cotton-
wadded, baggy pants, and Chinese shoes.   Only his fair
complexion and blue eyes showed his Anglo-Saxon
descent.   Thirty feet away he would attract no attention
from a Chinese crowd.   As for me, they could see I was
a "foreign devil" a half-mile away; and as we passed
through the small streets of the suburbs the urchins
caught sight of me blocks away, and hastened after us,
shouting "See! see! A foreign devil! A foreign
devil!"   A great deal of the abuse we endured during

that trip was no doubt due to my stubbornness in wearing "foreign" (American) clothing; but my companion
never once alluded to it, and never once said, "I told
you so."

I felt rejoiced when we at last passed through the
suburb gates and could leave those shouting young
hoodlums behind.   Our barrow-men, scantily clad, were
shivering with cold as we came up to where they were
awaiting us, and seemed glad that we were to start off
at once, as the exercise would soon put them in a glow.
I clambered up on top of my bedding on the right side;
Mr. Bergen did the same on the left.   "Zoah," we both
say in concert, and off we go at the dizzy rate of three
miles per hour.   The wind was blowing, directly in our
faces, a regular gale; so much so as to render conversation very uncomfortable, and so, after a few attempts,
we lapsed into silence.   The longer I sat, the colder I
became.   My legs, stretched out in front of me, allowed
the keen wind to blow up my pantaloons in such manner
as to speedily insure their freezing.   On glancing at my
companion's legs, I was disgusted to see how comfortable they looked, incased in those heavily-wadded pantaloons, tied closely at the ankles and effectually preventing
the ingress of wind.   I bit my lip and said nothing, but
mentally allowed that the next time I came out in
winter I would wear that kind of pants.

After an hour's travel we came to a fork in the road,
where there was what I took to be a sign-post, and so
remarked; but as we got closer to it I saw it was a
small wicker-basket, placed on a post, with an inscription over the top.   Mr. Bergen, who had also been
watching the same object, exclaimed, "Well!   I de-
clare!   It's a head!"   We stopped the barrow, and,

dismounting, walked up to the post. Sure enough, inside the wicker-cage or basket was a man's head. While I was noting the age of the party and the apparent method of decapitation my friend was reading the inscription above, and when he finished announced that the man had been decapitated three days previously for highway robbery committed at this spot a few months before, and that his head had been brought to the place of his crime and exposed to the public as a warning to others. The barrow-men had sat down beside the barrow when we left it and coolly lit their pipes, merely glancing at the cage, and smiling at our apparent curiosity in walking twenty feet from the road to look at it. " Tsei " (thief) sententiously remarked the eldest man, between two puffs of smoke, as we returned. " There are not many this winter," he continued, taking the pipe from his mouth ; " but two years ago every road leading from Chinanfu had those things placed along them, and some right close to the city-wall, too." " Pu ts'woa," (no mistake) chimed in the second man.

Getting down and moving about had warmed my nearly frozen ankles a little, and so I proposed walking awhile. Telling the barrow-men to follow, we walked along the narrow pathway, through fields of frozen broom-corn stalks, for about five miles. During this walk I saw the advantage of the thick Chinese soles of the shoes Mr. Bergen wore, as well as his wadded-cotton socks, over the shoes of thick, hard leather and comparatively thin soles I wore. Resolution No. 2 followed, viz., next time I will wear Chinese shoes.

We had been gradually drawing nearer a cone-shaped mountain, rising alone from the surrounding plain, and were now at its very foot and passing around it to reach the ferry over the Yellow River. "This cone is called 'Hua Shan' (flower mountain)," said Mr. Bergen; "though why I never could find out, as I have never seen a flower growing upon it even in summer-time." It was past noon when we arrived at the bank of the river. Only a little mat-shed—which was nearly blown down by the violence of the wind—and the cessation of the road gave evidence that this was the ferry. No boat was visible, either on this side or directly across; but, on closer inspection, we discovered the clumsy flat-boat, used as a ferry, to be a half-mile below on the opposite side, having just crossed with a cart and team of mules as passengers. The river at this point was a quarter of a mile wide, and, owing to the melting of a recent heavy fall of snow, was swollen and rapid. When a boat left one side it would be carried a half-mile down stream before the opposite side could be touched. Then the crew of four men would take a rope and pull the boat up to the landing-place, discharge cargo, and re-enact the same performance on the other side. We stood an hour in the cold, with no shelter, watching the boat, at first half a mile below us, pulled slowly to a corresponding point on the opposite bank; then, after it was unloaded and reloaded from that side, start toward us, and be swept a half-mile down on our side. Of course, much time is wasted by this primitive method of crossing rivers; but the Chinese are never in a hurry, and do not mind half a day lost at a ferry they could cross in three minutes, especially as they know nothing of the ferry-boats of modern times. "Have they no bridges?" some one asks. Yes; some very good ones over small streams; and, indeed, there used to be, many

5

years ago, a fine bridge across the Yellow River, opposite the city of Chee Ho, but the river has swept all
but a few of the stone piers away, and in this age of
decay no spirit of enterprise demands its rebuilding.

Just before we embarked on the ferry a wheelbarrow
arrived, conveying two prisoners, chained by the feet together, and in charge of a constable, whose only badge of
office was a black-painted stick, like a thick walking-cane.
These poor fellows had but little clothing on, and nothing to sit upon but the bare boards of the wheelbarrow.
Their heads and faces were unshaven and dirty; a look
of apathetic despair sat upon their countenances. When
the barrow stopped they arose and hobbled, as best they
could in their manacled feet, onto the boat, and, without
a word, seated themselves, shivering, upon the floor.
As I looked at the poor wretches, I thought, " No matter
what your crime, to-day's ride in the cold, dressed as you
are, would be ample punishment."

We crossed without accident, and, upon landing on
the north side, hastened on as rapidly as possible,
hoping to reach a village called Chu Ma Tien by dark.
In this village there were several inns, the only place
short of the city of Chi Yang where such a luxury (?)
was obtainable. Owing to the head-wind and our
long detention at the river, however, it soon became
apparent that we could not reach the village ahead
that night. Besides, we had eaten only a luncheon
on the barrow since starting, and now darkness was
coming on and we and our barrow-coolies were tired,
cold, and hungry. What was to be done? No house
was left standing inside the north bank of the river.
Only mat-sheds existed along the bank from time to
time, with the north side made of adobe-brick to bet-

ter break the force of the wind. We were traveling entirely on the river-bank, which was a raised levee, some twelve feet above the surrounding country, that resembled a barren marsh. As we passed these mat-dwellings the proprietors would frequently come out and ask us to stop for the night; but still we pushed on, in hopes of finding some more substantial dwelling.

At last the barrow-men declared they could wheel no farther, and Mr. Bergen reluctantly consented to stop at the next shed that presented itself. It was a full mile after he had thus decided before we found one, and I was heartily glad to see a large room, three sides of adobe-brick, roofed with corn-stalks, which an abrupt turn in the bank suddenly made visible. Our barrow was wheeled right into the only room, to find three other barrows and about twenty men already in the same room. A bright fire of corn-stalks lit up one end of the room, where, by the smell of frying onions, we could tell supper was in process of cooking. A rickety table, a chair with no back, and an extra-large platform of adobe-brick, covered by mats, for a bed, comprised the only furniture the room afforded. I soon found that the corn-stalk fire gave light, but very little heat, as inside this miserable apology for shelter the temperature was the same as outside. The wind, however, did not penetrate the adobe-wall, and so it was somewhat better than outside. The door-way we were obliged to leave open to let the smoke out, as there was no chimney. "Never mind," said my friend, noticing my disconsolate expression; "wait until we get some hot tea and a dish of scrambled eggs, and you will feel warmed up and all right." Our intrusion caused the guests already assembled to draw together in one end of the room, nearer the fire, allowing us to remain by ourselves at the other side. Our barrow-men were eagerly questioned as to who we were, what was our business, and where were we going.

"We might as well spread our beds on the kang while the landlord is cooking our eggs," said Mr. Bergen. Then he commenced pulling the quilts and comfortables out of the long bag which had served him as a seat during the day. "You may sleep next the wall, Doctor, as doubtless all this company will crowd on the kang to-night; and, as I don't mind sleeping next a China-man, it will be easier for you until you are broken in." I thanked him, and, laying down a goat-skin with long fur to sleep upon, arranged my comfortables and blankets on top for covers. "Where shall we place our clothes when we undress?" I asked. "Oh! we just lay them on top of us," he replied. "You won't find it any too warm with all you can get on you by morn-ing." Our obliging landlord gave up to us the rickety table, while the less honorable guests ate in a group from a pot placed in the centre of the room on the ground. Our supper consisted of a dish of scrambled eggs with onion finely chopped up in them, some bread called "kuo ping," resembling hard-tack, and a pot of hot tea, to which we added a few teaspoonfuls of condensed milk. Although this could not be called a feast, it supplied the necessary nourishment, and, above all, it was hot. My fingers were nearly frozen stiff, and I made such awkward efforts to hold the chopsticks, and with such poor suc-cess, that I finally gave them up and used my penknife and fingers, much to the amusement of the other guests, who from time to time came and stood beside us, watch-ing us eat.

We hastily finished our meal, and, after drinking

three cups of hot condensed milk, I became somewhat thawed and managed to find my pipe and some
fragrant Durham tobacco, which made me feel almost
comfortable. My short-stemmed pipe immediately caused
a great amount of comment, and the group around the
pot, having demolished its contents, now surrounded
me and overwhelmed me with questions, none of
which I understood. Mr. Bergen came to my rescue
and told them my pipe was of wood, that it would not
burn away, that it did not burn my mouth, that I
smoked tobacco much the same as theirs (which same I
deny), that I was a man same as they, that I could talk,
that my language was different from theirs, that in time
I would speak their language, that I had come to cure
their sick, and ever so many other things, all in answer
to the questions they in turn asked. These men were
all going the same way as ourselves, and promised to
keep us company on the morrow. Most of them were
small farmers who had been to the city of Chinanfu on
foot, and, returning, were belated, as was our case. A
few were coolies with barrow-loads of merchandise con-
signed to business-men in Chi Yang. They doubtless
were willing to chat all night, but we were very tired,
and about nine o'clock, getting quite cold, went to bed
for warmth. Mr. Bergen disrobed to his underwear, but
I only removed my overcoat, coat and vest, and shoes,
placing each of these articles, as removed, upon the top
of my covering. A group of men stood around me
watching me, much to my discomfort; but there was no
help for it, so I bore it patiently and slept none the worse
for it. I slept well until dawn, but awoke feeling chilly
and stiff.

My friend said he felt as bright as a dollar. He

gave orders to the landlord, sleeping on the floor or ground on the other side of the room, to get us some hot water at once, and by the time we were dressed a pot of hot tea awaited us. Not waiting for any further aliment, we paid our score of twenty cents for lodging and supper, and started out in the cold to pursue our journey, expecting to breakfast at Chu Ma Tien, some five miles farther on. We were pleased to find there was no wind blowing, and consequently did not suffer as much with the cold as on the previous day. An hour after sunrise we left the river-bank a half-mile to the south, and entered the village, which boasted of an inn, for breakfast. Only a dozen houses remained of two hundred formerly comprising this village, and these, owing to a higher knoll of ground, escaped the flood of the previous summer. We were shown into one of the two rooms composing the inn, and were quite pleased to note it had two good chairs and a table, besides a kang covered with a clean mat. Our breakfast was not long cooking, and with hearty appetites, encouraged by our walk from the starting-place, we enjoyed the fried pork and onions, hot sweet potatoes, cabbage-soup, and hot tea, which comprised the entire bill of fare the inn afforded.

While eating, the news had spread through the remaining houses in the village that a " foreign devil" was in the place; consequently, the little court-yard speedily filled with men, women, and children anxious to get a look at me. They scarcely noticed my companion, who was as much a devil as myself, but who in dress at least resembled themselves. My narrow pants struck them as exceedingly ludicrous, and many of them asked Mr. Bergen if I was not very cold, and why I did not tie my pants at the bottom to keep the wind out. Youngsters would point out my peculiarities to each other, and then burst out laughing; so that, try as I might to look unconcerned, I felt my face flush, and was extremely anxious to get away. I began to heartily wish I had taken advice and worn a suit of native clothes. We heard no bad language until we had seated ourselves again on the barrow and had left the village several hundred yards behind. Then, in chorus, all the young rapscallions of the village yelled out after us, " Foreign devil! Foreign devil! Foreign devil!" as long as we could hear. I wanted to go back and clean out the town, but my companion only smiled and said, " Oh! don't mind them; boys will be boys." A sharp turn in the road soon hid the village from view, and the path led us back to the river-bank again.

At noon we entered the rather dilapidated gate-way of the city of Chi Yang. This city, formerly one of the best hsien cities in the province, has, owing to the Yellow River floods and consequent impoverishment of the whole district, become one of the poorest. The wall is full of breaks, and there is a general air of decay about the place that is not unusual to Chinese cities. Business seemed nearly entirely suspended. On the main street a few small clothing-stores, several junk-shops, some " fan p'u tzus," or food-shops, and the inevitable cash-shop still struggled for existence, but the character of the goods displayed gave evidence of the limited buying capacity of the citizens. Many villages of a few hundred souls have more and better shops than this once thrifty city of Chi Yang. We entered the only inn still open to the public and obtained a fairly good meal of chopped-up beef, fried cabbage, with garlic, fried eggs, and momo. This last is a steam-baked bread, in form of rolls, which when fresh is very palatable. A crowd of men and boys gathered in the court-yard and watched us eat, commenting freely upon our appearance, manners, etc. I grew morbidly sensitive to these comments, especially as they all took the same general direction of questioning if I were not very cold, and why I did not tie my pants at the bottom to keep the wind out. Then, too, they insisted on calling my beard yellow, while I had always imagined it a beautiful chestnut-brown. I inwardly called them a set of color-blind idiots. I have since learned that they make no distinction of brown and yellow. Hair which is not jet-black or gray is called "huang" (yellow), unless, indeed, it is red, in which case it is called "hung" (red).

At last our own and our barrow-men's appetites were satisfied, and, although very cold, we started out on the last stretch of our journey, our destination being but twelve miles, or thirty-five li, farther on. It was near dusk as we reached the village of An Chia Miao, a quarter of a mile to the left of the north bank of the river. We went at once to the house of a farmer of Mr. Bergen's acquaintance, and were in Chinese fashion warmly welcomed. I was introduced to Mr. Li Ts'ang Hai and his brother, men of about forty-eight and fifty years of age, respectively.

This village had suffered less with the floods than most of those in the immediate vicinity, and so all of the houses remained standing, though many showed the saturation of water for three feet above the ground, in the adobe-brick, of which they were all constructed. Mr. Li, being the wealthiest man in the village, possessed a comfortable adobe dwelling of twelve rooms, built around a square court, in which several donkeys, a pig, and some chickens roamed around, looking vainly on the frozen ground for a nourishing blade of fodder or grain of corn. We were led at once into the guest-room, a twelve-by-sixteen-feet apartment, with a door that would not shut tight, and windows from which the paper-panes were missing. The floor was of soil beaten hard, and the furniture consisted of a table, two chairs, and the adobe kang, covered with a new mat. Our bedding was at once brought in and deposited on this kang, and then all our host's family, consisting of his mother, wife, sister, sister-in-law, and numerous nephews and nieces, crowded in and wished us "hao," and immediately fell to asking Mr. Bergen the stereotyped questions,—if I was not cold, etc.

The old mother, a real nice old lady, with gray hair and a kindly old face full of wrinkles, came alongside me on the kang, and, in a voice full of sympathy, said: "Ain't you cold? Your pants look so thin." I assured her, with my teeth chattering, that I was quite warm; but she did not believe me, and gave an order to one of her grand-children, which resulted in a brass basin of charcoal-fire being brought in and placed on the table before me to warm my hands by.

Mr. Bergen at once entered into conversation about the crops, floods, condition of the village, etc., with a facility which caused me to envy him. However, he could not absorb the attention of the roomful of Lis, try as he might. My pants were too attractive. First, old Mrs. Li, then middle Mrs. Li, then all the young Lis edged up and felt the bottom of my pants and commented on them, and wound up by declaring that, as they were wool, they must be warmer than they looked, and that if I tied the bottoms they thought I might keep warm.

Our host went out after awhile and came back with several sheets of stout paper and a pot of flour-paste, with which he proceeded to repane the windows, greatly to my comfort, as the wind was rising every moment, and the three-inch crack in the door seemed sufficient for ventilation. Stoves are unknown; the cotton-wadded clothing, although it makes a man look five times as large as he is, keeps out the cold. In the bitterest weather a pan of charcoal is lit to warm the hands and feet by, and a little straw is always burned in the kang before retiring, heating it for the night. Our barrow and coolies were sent to a small inn at the other end of the village and told to remain there during our stay in the village.

After half an hour's chat the female portion of the family withdrew to prepare a meal for us, and the men and boys, with the boys of all the neighbors' families, took their place as our entertainers. A Chinese bean-oil lamp was lit and set on the table, and the men all lit their pipes, and soon the little room was so filled with smoke that from where I sat upon the kang the little light looked like a steamer-lamp in a fog. As there were only two chairs in the room, Mr. Bergen occupied one and Mr. Li the other; the villagers and boys sat squatting around on the floor. In a remarkably short space of time a boy entered to tell the villagers to clear out, as food was ready and the teachers were tired and must eat. Unlike the crowds at the inns, they all arose, and, politely saying " We will see you again," they went out. Then a steaming-hot bowl of " mien" was placed before Mr. Bergen, followed by three others; two more chairs minus backs were brought in, and I was invited to sit up and partake, with Mr. Li and his brother, of the viands the "poor state" of his larder afforded.

Mr. Li, being a Christian, said grace before his meal, but I was not sufficiently educated to catch the words he used.   Although I detest "mien," it was hot and I was cold, therefore I made haste to put as much of it into my interior as the space would accommodate.   Afterward, when the fried cabbage and scrambled eggs came along, I did likewise, until I finally felt both full and comfortably warm.   All this time I kept my overcoat and hat on, as did all the party.   A Chinaman never removes his hat in winter from the time he places it on his head in the morning until he retires at night.   When we pushed back our chairs, after being urged again and again to eat more by the hospitable Mr. Li, the dishes were removed and the pipes again lit, and conversation flowed smoothly on again.   Unfortunately, I could only answer about one in ten of the questions addressed me, my answer for the remainder being the same sentence, "Wo pu tung tei" (I don't understand you).

Various neighbors dropped in during the course of the evening, who each in turn nodded to Mr. Li and then squatted on the floor.   Some were brought over to my end of the room and introduced.   One of these, I was told, was the "ti fang," or policeman of the village, and tax-collector for several smaller villages in the neighborhood.   Toward bed-time quite a stir occurred in the crowd, and a personage of importance was evidently being admitted.   This proved the case.   The boys all arose and stood aside as a man about thirty-five, with a long, dirty, blue-cotton gown, entered and was introduced as the village-teacher, Mr. Ts'ao.   His manner was very important, and he addressed every one in a most patronizing style. I took a dislike to him at once. I did not know then what an important man the village-teacher is, nor how universal was this mixture of pride and condescension among them as a class. He remained but a short time, and after his departure our considerate host dismissed the company by saying, " The teachers have come far and are in need of repose ; return to your homes and allow them to sleep, and call again on the morrow and see them." They bade us good-night, as did our host and his brother, and, getting out our bedding the same as we did in the inns, we were soon sound asleep.

In the morning when we arose we again collected and restored our blankets in the bag used for that purpose, as, the kang being used as a general sitting-place, they would otherwise have occupied too much room. Guests in China always bring their own bedding when visiting, no matter whether the host be poor or wealthy. Relatives visiting relatives, even, always carry their own bedding with them. A basin of hot water was brought us to bathe with, but no towel, we being expected to furnish our own. After a wash, a breakfast of hot millet-gruel, boiled eggs, and momo was served; our visitors, more numerous than the night before, were now re-admitted. The ground being frozen, the farmers were all unoccupied, and our chamber never lacked a full attendance. They were all clad alike ; coarse, blue, cotton-wadded trousers, very baggy, tied at the ankles with a strip of tape an inch wide called a " tai zu," and held up at the waist by a circular sash of strong blue cotton, or in some cases by a belt of ordinary rope. At their belts hung a bag of tobacco and a flint and steel for striking fire. On their heads they wore the ordinary round, black hat of coarse felt. Shoes of coarse blue cotton and stockings of dirty white cotton completed the attire. Many of these stockings looked as though they had never seen water, and as Mr. Bergen assured me most of the men only owned one pair, which they wore all winter, you may imagine their color.

In the afternoon we walked around the village; every one who met us bowed politely and said " Hao ?" (Are you well ?). On the outskirts of the village was a small burying-ground, and I noticed a number of little graves that looked as though they had recently been torn open. My companion informed me that the babies were buried here, and only covered with sufficient dirt to hide the body from sight. As no coffin is used, the body is dug up at night and eaten by the dogs. The villagers intend it thus, for, they say, " An evil spirit inhabited the child's body, otherwise it would not have died so young. If the dogs eat it, the bad spirit enters a dog and cannot again enter another child who may be born to the same parents." Outside of every city or village in the North may be seen one of these infant burying-grounds,—simply a number of little holes in which the infant is deposited, and a little loose dirt to cover with. I found this village to consist of about one hundred adobe houses, an inn, and a school-house. Only ten boys attended school, the rest of the young male population being left to grow up in ignorance. When I asked why all the smaller boys did not go to school, I was informed that if they did their parents would have to help contribute to the teacher's salary, and they could not afford it. The teacher received but three dollars a month for teaching ten boys, and had to board himself, too. Yet, teaching is considered the best profession in China. There are no such things as public schools in the country.

When we returned from our walk, numerous patients were waiting to be seen; so, using Mr. Bergen as interpreter, I commenced examination and dispensation work, and kept it up until dark. Dyspepsia was the principal ailment, with worms, neuralgias, and chronic rheumatisms, eye and ear troubles, and a sprinkling of most everything recorded in the chapter on diseases common to China. A second day followed much as the first, and so for five days Mr. Li's house became a free dispensary, greatly to his delight. He seemed intensely interested in the treatment of every case, and wanted to know if I thought him too old to study the foreign system of medicine.

At last my medicine ran out, and Mr. Bergen, having completed his parishional duties, we returned to Chinanfu. Our home journey was a repetition of the outward one,—cold to freezing all the time. With my foreign dress to repel strangers, and my incapacity to talk much, except through an interpreter, I felt my trip had only been a success inasmuch as it showed me how best to approach the people. For eight months after my return to the city I studied every day with the assistance of Mr. T'an in the morning, devoting the afternoons to dispensary patients and city practice.

In September, 1886, I came to the conclusion to try the native dress and again visit the country. I did so; discarded every Western garment, and adopted that of the Celestial. It was a decided success; everywhere I was treated better and bad language was almost unheard, besides being better suited to the climate than American clothing. In company of my medical assistant I revisited Chi Yang and many other villages, spending days at a time in the house of some hospit-

A Native Physician and his Family.

able villager, while I treated the sick in his and the surrounding villages. The language became gradually more fluent, and by and by thoughts suggested themselves in Chinese as readily as English. For four years I wore the native dress, and found it not only more convenient in the country, but also in the city of Chinanfu. Rich mandarins became my friends and visiting acquaintances, who would never have invited me to their houses dressed in American clothes. I cannot say I like the dress as well as my native costume, but I feel that to it I owe much of the information acquired while living in the interior of China, amongst the most exclusive and uncommunicative people on earth. In the open seaports it is unnecessary, even objectionable, to wear the Chinese dress. In the interior the experience of all who have tried it is, that it greatly facilitates communication with the people, and lessens the disrespectful and abusive language showered upon the " yang kuei tzu " (foreign devil) who promenades abroad in the costume of the West.

CHAPTER V.

THE Northern Chinaman is as different from the Southern as the Englishman is from the Frenchman. He is taller, darker, or more copper-colored, and of heavier build. His disposition is more sluggish; he retaliates more slowly when injured, and is of less finely organized nervous make-up. Not that he is less courageous; in fact, I think, if anything, he is more so; but he lacks that volatile, nervous—fiery, you might almost say—disposition that is so characteristic of the Cantonese. His very language is different and much more musical and pleasant to the ear, lacking the abrupt and guttural sounds of the South, which are so harsh and grating. It is true the written language is the same, and the same mysterious-looking symbols represent his thoughts when writing, but he pronounces these characters differently and with a much more musical intonation. Some people seem perfectly amazed when told that a man from Canton would not be at all understood in the North, but such is undoubtedly the case. I have acted as interpreter between a Cantonese and a Mandarin-speaking man on several occasions while in charge of the wounded at the P'ing Tu mining accident. A Canton man was berating a Northern man for his stupidity in not doing as he had directed him, not a word of which the latter understood Upon my arrival on the scene the Northern man asked me, in a piteous tone of voice, what the Southerner was talking about. The Cantonese, who had resided in San Francisco some years, could talk a little English, and he conveyed to me in English his instructions to his coun tryman, who, upon my repeating them to him in Mandarin, instantly complied with his superior's commands.

A Chinaman, wherever he is, is possessed of a great amount of pride,—insufferable pride, the foreigner calls it. It is more evinced toward the foreigner, whom he has been taught to regard as an ignoramus and a " foreign devil," than toward his own people. The bearing of the students at the examinations toward the shop-keepers of their own nation, and all others who are not, as they suppose, of their own literary excellence, is haughty and offensive in the extreme ; so much so as to incur the dislike, and even hatred, of the shop-keepers, who, among other names, call them " pu lun li ti's " and " wu chih ti ren," which mean men who act unreasonably and men who know nothing.   A Chinaman's pride is usually in proportion to his literary attainments, and it takes but very little education to give him a vast amount of pride.

A gentleman who has taken his " shiu tsai," or first degree, is looked up to as a marvel of learning, having studied the works of Confucius and Mencius, the great learning and the doctrine of the mean, and been to the examinations ; but if you were to ask this learned gentleman the boundaries of China, the direction of England, or the distance of the sun from the earth, he would be obliged to answer he did not know, if he answered at all.   Most likely he would give you a supercilious look over the top of his big goggles (worn for style) and pass on without answering you.   I have often enjoyed the discomfiture of some of these learned specimens, when, after a series of ordinary questions, none of which they could answer, I would remark, " Well ! well ! Why, all of our ten-year-old boys in America know little facts like these."

I remember once, when sitting on a wheelbarrow by the roadside while my barrow-men were resting, two literary men with long gowns and goggles stepped up to me, and without any ceremony or address, which from their own point of view is excessively rude, put their faces in between my face and the book (an English novel) I was reading. I drew my head back in surprise, but said nothing. After scanning the book curiously front and back, and looking in vain for some familiar character, one turned to the other and said, " Lien i ko tzu wo pu yen tei." (I do not recognize a single character.) They were both thunderstruck when I quietly said, in Chinese, " Then your learning is very limited." The barrow-men and by-standers joined in a hearty laugh at their expense, and they moved sheepishly away.

The Chinese all have a great respect for written characters, and will not put to a dishonorable or dirty use any paper bearing written or printed characters upon it. So great is this esteem that there are societies in Canton, Shanghai, and perhaps other cities, that have paid employés to collect all such paper blowing about the streets and burn it, for fear it will be put to some dishonorable use and their sages who invented the characters dishonored. This is one of their notions that is fast becoming obsolete. The servants and teachers constantly associated with foreigners soon lose that exalted estimation they once held for the sanctity of the Chinese characters.

Perhaps there is no other nation in which the desire for a male descendant is so universal as in China. Every man longs to have one or more sons; daughters are by the majority looked upon as a burden, if not a curse. They are reared only to become members of another family upon their marriage; but sons remain at home, work the ground or succeed in the business or profession, perpetuate the name, and, greatest of all, worship at the grave of their paternal ancestor, after he has " passed over," or " left the world," as they designate a man's death.   A woman who bears only daughters is looked upon with disfavor by her husband, and may consider herself fortunate if he does not abuse and maltreat her.

Infanticide of female infants, reported as a frequent practice in Southern China, must be rare in the North, as I never heard of a single instance of it.   The girls are often neglected, ill fed, and poorly clothed, while their brothers receive every gift the fond father can lavish upon them.   Even the mothers often despise their female offspring and abuse them beyond belief.   Occasionally this is not the case, some families treating their male and female children equally well, and in some rare cases even allowing the girls to learn to read and write with their brothers.   If an official finds, after some years of wedded life, his children are all girls, he will take one or more concubines to bear him an heir.   Should one of these become mother of a male child she is greatly exalted, and, although during the wife's life-time she can never be considered the T'ai T'ai, or wife, yet she has much influence with the lao yeh, and is a source of constant envy to the unfortunate wife.

I have often had beggars run after me crying, " Give me a cash, *old teacher*, and your wife will bear you a son next year."   Upon the birth of a son all the neighbors and immediate relatives of the party so blessed will hasten to congratulate him upon his good fortune. If a girl is born, either no notice is taken of the event or the nearest of kin will condole with the father and wish him " better luck next time." Sons are not always the comfort and joy anticipated at their birth, however; for in China, as in other countries, they often turn out badly, and are a source of much anxiety to their father. This is especially the case with the sons of officials, who, having plenty of money, surrounded by flatterers and underlings, are led into scrapes that disgrace both themselves and their parents.

When a son marries he usually brings his wife to live under the paternal roof, and his brothers do likewise; so that it is frequently the case that three or four families live in the same house. There does not occur the same amount of disputation and wrangling under this arrangement as would occur in Western lands, because, owing to the patriarchal system of government, the father remains the head of the house during his life-time, and is the supreme power in the family from whose decision there is no appeal. After his death, should the family remain together, the eldest son takes his place. The wives are all subject to their mother-in-law, who usually makes life as uncomfortable for them as possible. Their only satisfaction is to nurse up their wrongs until the day when they have daughters-in-law of their own, upon whom they can wreak their stored-up vengeance. When a girl is married you never hear any one make remarks about the kind of a husband she married, but every one says either she is going to a good mother-in-law or her mother-in-law is a bad woman,—expressing the fact that her life will be more what her mother-in-law makes it than what her husband makes it. A son in America becomes " his own man " upon completing his twenty-first year, but in China, during the life-time of his father, he is never his own man. His marriage is arranged for him without his having any voice in the matter, his earnings are always his father's, and, should he acquire any property, it may be taken from him by his father's creditors to satisfy any outstanding debt of the old gentleman's.

To be a son with a bad or spendthrift father, in China, is more unfortunate than to be a father with a worthless or profligate son. If in a family of two brothers but one should be blessed with an only son, it is sometimes the case that this son, on arriving at manhood, will be given two wives, one of whom is supplied by the uncle and resides with his family, the other by the father and resides at the young man's home. He is expected to divide his time between the two homes: the offspring of the wife at his own home will be his father's descendants, the offspring of the wife at his uncle's, though his own children, will be considered his uncle's descendants. I know of just such a case in the P'ing Tu district. Should one of two brothers be blessed with sons and the other not, the fortunate one will often give one of his sons to his brother, in order that his grave shall not lack descendants to honor it, nor his tablet fail of worship at the New Year's time. Boys sometimes have their ears pierced, and are obliged to wear earrings, in order to fool the bad spirits into the belief that they are girls, and thus prevent their early decease; the parents believing that the spirits desire to take away those on whom their hearts are set rather than one of a despised sex.

The endurance of a Chinaman is something remarkable. On a poor diet he is capable of more outlay of strength than seems at a glance possible. Any one who has witnessed the barrow-men pushing along a load weighing from three to five hundred pounds, a distance of thirty miles per day, cannot but be struck with the wonderful endurance displayed by the men. I have traveled many miles upon wheelbarrows, and have seen thousands of men engaged in the "one-man-power transportation," yet, unto this day, I never cease to admire the patient, tireless energy of these poor creatures. They are usually the younger sons of an indigent farmer, whose land is insufficient to support himself and all his family, and so the younger sons are obliged to adopt this means to keep body and soul together. They are paid but ten or twelve cents a day, and with this they must manage to feed and clothe themselves. To be sure, their clothing is a small item : in summer it consists of a pair of cotton pants, costing, new, but fifteen cents; in winter, of a pair of pants lined with raw cotton, costing twenty-five cents, with a blouse of the same material, at about twice that sum,—always bought second-hand at the commencement of winter and pawned (if not completely worn-out) in the spring. Their life is one constant monotony of toil. If they are taken seriously ill, unless provided for by some charitable person, they die of starvation; for they have no means of saving, if they had the inclination. They rise in the morning from the ground or mat-kang of the cheapest of inns, where they spent the night, and proceed as far as three miles with their load before breaking their fast. Their first meal will consist of a pound and a half of hard bread, a radish, and two or three bowls of hot water, for which they will pay two and a half cents. They will then wheel three miles farther and stop again, for a few whiffs of tobacco from their little pipes and another bowl or two of hot water, at some convenient " k'ai shui p'u," or hot-water shop, for which they pay one cash, equivalent to one-tenth of a cent, per bowl.   At the next stopping-place, about the same distance away, another smoke and a bowl or two of hot millet-gruel are indulged in, at an expense of three or four cash per bowl.   At noon a rest of an hour is taken, and some fried cabbage or other vegetable, with bread, are ingested, costing about three cents.   Throughout the afternoon, about every ten li, or three miles, a halt is made for smoking and water-drinking, with occasionally a bowl of millet-gruel, called "hsi fan," or a radish, or cucumber, until night comes on, and the poor fellows, completely fagged out, seek the mat-shelter of some miserable inn in which to pass the night.   Here they spend the remainder of their day's allowance, usually clubbing together to buy a huge pot of " mien t'iao tzu," which is a dough made of flour and water, cut into thin strips, and boiled with a little salt, occasionally having an onion or two in it.   If, perchance, there are a few cash left, the now refreshed coolies will sit up and gamble it away, or win enough to buy a few ounces of " shao chiu " (impure alcohol), which they drink hot before retiring.   You would be surprised to find that there are white-haired men following this vocation, who have worked at it as many as forty years.   They never marry, and, as a rule, do not care for the opposite sex.   They are too tired after their day's work to indulge the sexual appetite, and as soon as their evening meal is finished, and their money gone, forget their fatigue in sleep.

It is not only the barrow-men who display this wonderful endurance.   The muleteers, who follow the carts, donkeys, and pack-mules a distance of from thirty to forty miles per day; the "pao hsin ti," or mail-runner, who travels across the province with from twenty to forty pounds' weight on his shoulder; the traveling peddler, with his heavy pack; and many others, none of whom receive at most fifteen cents per day, all manifest a quality of endurance not, as far as I know, found anywhere but in China. They are called coolies by the foreigner, the derivation of the word being the two Chinese words, "k'u li" (bitter strength), meaning the strength put forth in bitterness, or by necessity of poverty. Often, at the dispensary, when I have asked a man what he did for a living, he would reply, "Mai li ch'i" (I sell my strength).

These coolies are so constantly ill-treated that their natures become warped, and they naturally take a pessimistic view of life; oftentimes they are so stupid, pig-headed, and obstinate, that it is next to impossible to get them to obey you; but sometimes they are very decent fellows, and, when treated kindly, will evince a thoughtfulness for your comfort, and care for your interests, as pleasant as it is unexpected.

I must say, I have a great liking for these wheel-barrow-men especially. Often, after a hard day's journey, I have left my upper room at the inn and gone down front, where the wheelbarrow-men were collected, to spend an hour or two chatting, or, even smoke a pipe with them. I have always found them respectful and full of information, which they were glad to impart, about the country we were passing through, the inns best to stop at, and the condition of the roads.

Lying is a vicious habit, universally practiced all over the empire. It is regarded as a necessary talent in

Peking Cart.

business operations to lie well. " Squeezing," or "taking commissions " is as common. The usual plan of operations is: the purchaser of any article for another reports the price from 10 to 300 per cent. higher than he paid for it, and keeps the difference. If he thinks his employer wants the article very badly, and there is a scarcity of supply, his commission will be inordinate. I will give an example. Coming home from the hospital one day in the spring, I noticed green peas on the market, the first of the season. Upon my arrival home I called my cook, and, informing him where they could be found, directed him to go buy some at once for dinner. He took his basket and went out at once, but returned in five minutes with a rueful countenance, saying he dared not purchase at the figure demanded, viz., four hundred and fifty small cash a pound (equal to twenty-two and a half cents.) Knowing such prices were never asked for peas, I suspicioned the cook of a desire to swindle heavily; so I told him not to mind it, but to go into the kitchen and prepare dinner. I then called my old gate-keeper, a man over sixty years of age, and too stupid to be much of a thief, and, giving him a string of cash, told him to go buy me two pounds of peas. " Buy them as cheaply as you can, but bring me two pounds at any cost." On his return with the peas, he told me he had been obliged to pay one hundred cash per pound. I sent them into the kitchen and made his cookship nearly wild by the discovery of his rascality. He beat the old man severely for daring to buy without first communicating with him, and received his discharge summarily.

All business of importance is transacted through a middle man. A purchase of property without a middle man is not legal. Any one can act in the capacity of

middle man; no special requirements are necessary. A
Chinaman is never in a hurry. No matter what the
business in hand, there is always time to smoke or chat.
It is very exasperating to the foreigner, used to having
things put through in a hurry, to do business with the
Chinese. Americans, especially, find this trait of the
Oriental exceedingly vexatious. For instance, you are
going on a journey; you have bargained the day before
with a cart-hong to send you a cart and pack animals
for baggage promptly at 8 A.M. At the appointed time,
having eaten an early breakfast, you are all in readiness,
but no cart appears. You send your servant to the hong
and he soon re-appears, saying the " chang-kuei ti," or
head man, says they are coming right away. You light
your cigar and walk impatiently up and down, looking
from time to time at your watch. Nine o'clock, still no
cart. You send again to the hong; same reply. Ten
o'clock, your man comes back from the hong, this time
saying the head man regrets very much that his carts
have not come in from where he had expected them, but
he has sent a man to see where they are, and as soon as
they arrive he will get you started. At noon you are
told the carts have just arrived at the hong, but the
animals are hungry and must be fed before they can go
out again; two hours will be required for feeding. You
now hope to get off by two o'clock. At three your cart
arrives, but no pack-mules. You can take your choice:
go on, and let your trunks follow next day, or keep your
cart on your premises all night, get your pack-mules
together, and make an early start in the morning.

After many such experiences you never expect to start
until you are actually in motion. A Chinese official once
told me that it might do very well for trains to start on

time in America, but they could not do it if railroads were inaugurated in China, " for," said he, " we couldn't get ready in time."   This procrastination is seen everywhere and in all sorts of business.   It is a particular feature in their diplomacy.   The ministers and ambassadors of England, Russia, and the United States storm, rave, and threaten the Tsung Li Yamen in Peking; but the wily old mandarins smile in their capacious sleeves, and by excuse after excuse, based upon the flimsiest pretexts, delay and often foil the best diplomats of modern times.   There is no such thing as secrecy.   All public business is conducted with a roomful or courtful of underlings and yamen-runners standing around in full sight, listening. By paying the right man you can secure a full report of the most private business transacted in any of the yamens or bureaus.   Anybody's business is everybody's business. If you enter a shop to make a purchase, any passer-by who takes a notion to will stop, enter, look on, comment, and often assist either you or the shop-keeper in the transaction; but if a cart upsets or a wheelbarrow-man spills his load, not one of the crowd which collects will lend a hand to help the poor coolie.   His wreck may obstruct the street a half a day if some other coolie or carter does not make his appearance and render assistance.   Genuine sympathy is a very scarce article.   Good Samaritans are more rare even than in Palestine.

The Chinese have a great faculty for imitation, but cannot, even under stress of necessity, invent.   Give a carpenter a picture of a table, wardrobe, or any piece of furniture, let the carving be ever so intricate, still, when finished, the article will be an exact counterpart of the picture given him.   Brass-workers, silversmiths, and weavers all have the same faculty.   Give them but a

model and they will speedily reproduce it. Ask them
for an original design and they are unable to give it.
The cart, wheelbarrow, and boat of to-day are all of
the same model as they were a thousand or more years
ago.

The Chinese always congregate in villages, towns, or
cities. They never live in solitary dwellings on the
plains, or between villages. Their attachment to the
spot of their nativity is one of the strongest traits in
their characters. Every Chinaman desires to die in the
village where he was born, or, if from any cause beyond
his control he cannot come home to die, he will, if pecu-
niarily able, take measures to secure the transportation
of his remains to his home after his decease. Every
Pacific steamer returning to China carries the remains
of Chinese who have died in the United States back to
the land of their birth. The people, from the highest to
the lowest, evince a love of the lower animals. Birds
and dogs are the particular pets. It is a frequent sight
to see several well-dressed men sitting just outside the
gate of a village or city, near sundown, each holding a
bird-cage containing a lark or some other specimen of
the feathered tribe. They are giving the birds an airing,
and, as they sit smoking and discussing the merits of
their various pets, all cares are forgotten and they are
supremely happy. Some admire cats, and nourish a
great number of them. My next-door neighbor in
Chinanfu kept sixteen of these pets, and was in a perpetual state of fear lest I should shoot or poison some
of them, as I frequently promised him I would.

The Northern Chinese are not quarrelsome, and,
when they do get into a fight, usually make more noise
than injury. Slapping in the face, pulling the queue,

and scratching with their long nails is as far as they get in fisticuffs. A real knock-down and drag-out fight is the rarest of spectacles.

If you witness a row in the street, you can always know, without asking, the cause of it, viz., one party is in debt to the other, who has been trying to collect, and, not succeeding, has commenced a fight to call the attention of the neighborhood to the insolvent condition of the debtor. Women of the laboring classes often engage in street-fights; you can hear them for blocks away, and their language is of the foulest and most disgusting sort imaginable. They have no blasphemous profanity, as with us, but instead have a vocabulary of vulgarity which is, if anything, more shocking to hear. I have seen two old, gray-headed women standing opposite each other on the principal street of a city, with faces distorted by rage, shouting abuse at each other as fast as their tongues could work, surrounded by a crowd of men and boys, all of whom seemed tickled at the spectacle. Murders, except by highwaymen, are rare; suicides exceedingly frequent. Adultery, in spite of their seclusion of women, is far from rare. Theft is less common than in the United States. Embezzlement is the prevailing form of dishonesty, in which the Chinaman imitates the bank-president rather than the sneak-thief.

A Chinaman is born a gambler. No other race exhibits the same fondness for games of chance as the native of the flowery kingdom. Cards, dice, and wheels of fortune have served him in the past; but to-day, in the port cities, horse-racing and speculation are largely patronized, and in the interior the Manilla lottery finds a ready market for its seductive tickets.

CHAPTER VI.

HOME LIFE.

THE people of China may be as properly called the upper ten, the middle class, and the laboring class as the people of America, and it will suit my purpose better to describe them under these classifications.

First, then, the upper ten. By this term we consider all those having high official position and wealth. This would include the government officers of both military and civil degrees down to the magistrate of a "hsien," or district. Some of them are immensely wealthy, while others having a high rank in the service are possessed of comparatively small means. It also includes the members of their families, for frequently an official will have a dozen uncles, nephews, and cousins living with and dependent upon him who have no official rank, and may not even have a degree; yet during his life-time they are permitted to move in his circle of acquaintances. In event of his death or disgrace they have to shift for themselves, and are no longer recognized by the former splendid friends of their relative. Perhaps a description of the home of one of these official gentlemen will best illustrate the meaning of the "upper ten" of China.

Mr. Chang Shan Ma, with whom I am well acquainted, is a mandarin of the second rank who has been a Tao T'ai, and is entitled to wear a red button on his hat. This gentleman is tall, handsome, and inclined to corpulency; his moustache is thick and long, of a jet-black color, matching his luxuriant, silk-braided queue. He is possessed of ample means, and comes of good family. His residence in the provincial city of

(94)

Chinanfu is just east of the Governor's yamen, on a clean and tolerably wide street. He has three wives, and several children by each of them. When I first made his acquaintance he was about fifty years of age, but looked considerably younger. His residence, like all Chinese premises, consists of numerous separate buildings, arranged around small, vacant squares or courts. The front court contained three houses, each fitted up as a guest reception-room, but of different degrees of splendor, the upper house being the one in which he received his most honored guests,—those of equal or higher rank than himself. The furniture of this house, or rather room (for the building—thirty feet front by twelve feet deep—is but one room), was a "mu kang," or wooden platform, two feet high, eight feet front, and five feet deep, with carved front and varnished sides. The top was covered with red flannel, and in the centre sat a table, eight inches high and about eighteen inches wide, leaving sufficient space on either side for a guest to recline and take his opium from the little table. This "mu kang" was placed at the head or north end of the room. From it to the door on each side of the room are a half-dozen carved and varnished black chairs, with a small tea-table between each two. The walls are ornamented with scrolls in the several styles of Chinese penmanship, all describing the virtues and abilities of the head of the house. These scrolls have been presented to him by admiring friends, and are highly prized by Mr. Chang. Each chair has a red-flannel cushion, and each tea-table has a slip of red flannel covering the front and reaching to the brick floor. The two side-houses are somewhat smaller, and are used to receive guests of less distinction, and as dining-rooms, lounging-rooms, or business-rooms, as necessity dictates. Tradesmen or small officials are always seen by Mr. Chang in the lower rooms. Back of this court and to each side are two smaller courts, containing three small houses each, which lodge his secretaries, retainers, and the teacher of his children. Still back of this are the family quarters, divided into two courts, the second and third wives living in one, while the T'ai T'ai, or first wife, has a court to herself. Only this first wife is considered the wife, Mrs. Chang No. 2 and Mrs. Chang No. 3 being considered as concubines, as they really are. Mrs. Chang No. 1 is also of good family, equal to that of her husband, while the two later wives were taken to raise children, and are of humble parentage. The children of the concubines are called the children of the wife, and she has supreme control of them, the real mother being only a sort of wet-nurse.

There is in every household a great amount of wrangling and fighting amongst the women, with frequently suicides of the wives and concubines over this matter of control of the children, and from jealousy and anger. I venture to say there are very few Chinese officials having two or more wives who have never had at least one attempted, if not successful, suicide in their families. Mr. Chang's family is as peaceful as any where the polygamous relation is maintained, and yet I was told by his steward that No. 2 and No. 3 were constantly fighting. I have been called to numerous cases of suicide due to family quarrels among the upper ten. Sometimes it was the wife and sometimes the concubine who, from spite or jealousy, sought to destroy her life by taking opium. Mr. Chang has a separate room in front as his sleeping-apartment, but whenever he decides to pass the night with any one of his spouses, his retainers are directed to hang a pair of red-silk lanterns in front of that particular apartment; this notifies the inmate that she is to be honored by a visit from her lord on that evening, and also notifies the retainers not to enter those apartments without first knocking. The wife and concubines sometimes live on very good terms, and even go out visiting in company. On one occasion my wife was visited by four ladies named Mrs. Wu, being the first, second, third, and fourth wives, respectively, of Judge Wu, of Wen Shang hsien. Mr. Chang takes his meals in one of the front houses or reception-rooms with his immediate male relatives. Mrs. Chang eats with the maidens and smaller children, and the two concubines usually eat, each in her own apartments, waited upon by an old serving-woman called a "lao ma" (old mother).

Tao T'ai Chang has about thirty retainers and four serving-women, all of whom he feeds and clothes. His establishment is one of the best in the city, and he is known all over the province as a wealthy and able man. When visitors come to see him they are never permitted to see his wife, and when Lady Chang has visitors from among her friends and acquaintances (always feminine) they always arrive in closed sedan-chairs, which are carried into the female apartments and set down, and after the bearers have retreated the daintily-clad visitor emerges to be welcomed by Mrs. Chang, who sends word to Mr. Chang to make himself invisible until the lady has departed.

In the "Li Chi," or book of rites, the rules laid down for wealthy ladies read: "From their tenth year girls are not to be allowed to go out. A widow is to teach them obedience, tenderness, and good manners.

7

They are to be taught to work in hemp and linen, to manage silk-cocoons, to braid trimmings and fringes. They are to learn all kinds of women's work, and to make garments. They are to learn to look after the sacrifices, take charge of condiments and sauces, pickles, fruits, and meat. In all worship they are to assist at offerings before gods. In their fifteenth year they are to receive ornaments for the hair to show they are full-grown. In their twentieth year they are to be married, unless they are in mourning for a parent, in which case the marriage is to be deferred three years."

The lady has her female friends and relatives to dine with her occasionally, but the husband is under no circumstances permitted to make one of the party. Very few ladies of even the highest rank can read or write, and their life of enforced confinement is so very irksome that many take to the seductive opium-pipe simply to pass time away. My wife once asked a wealthy lady visitor, "What do you ladies do with yourselves if you don't read and can't go shopping?" "Why, we just eat and sleep," replied her guest; "only sometimes we have visitors, and then, too, we embroider a little and smoke the water-pipe; and, when things get too awfully dull, we fight among ourselves." Many ladies, in fact, most all of them, smoke the water-pipe; and, as it requires a great deal of manipulation for each puff of smoke obtained, this helps to consume many idle moments otherwise unendurable. They use a scented, aromatic tobacco in the water-pipe, which resembles ground-up brown paper, and is remarkably free from nicotine. The ideas of the Chinese upon the treatment of women and girls is very different from our own. Once when an old gentleman of my acquaintance was visiting me my little daughter, five years old, ran into the room, and, climbing up on my knee, kissed me. My visitor expressed his surprise, and remarked, " We never kiss our daughters when they are so large; we may when they are very small, but not after they are three years old," said he, " because it is apt to excite in them bad emotions, which young girls should not know. Young girls should be kissed by no man until they are married, and then, of course, only by their husbands," the old man concluded

This seems to me to be carrying the seclusion of women to a point too far to be anything but ridiculous. The Chinese men seem to have the idea that a woman is essentially bad, and only needs opportunity to prove it. Their system of concubinage is attended, in at least some instances, with bad results, directly due to adultery. A slighted concubine, or one who is not contented with the divided attentions of her lord, will choose from among his secretaries, or even servants, a mate for herself, and when her guilt is discovered she will take poison to escape the consequences of her unfaithfulness. Sometimes the first wife remains the only wife. This is especially likely to be the case if she is fortunate enough to bear sons to her lord. I remember a Mrs. Lieu, wife of Judge Lieu, of Chang Ping, who used to visit my wife, and whom I once attended. Her eyes would flash whenever she spoke about the polygamous relations of her people. " I would just like to see my ' lao yeh ' take another wife. I would make it hot for him and her. He dare not; for haven't I borne him five of the finest boys in this city ?" If they had been girls I am afraid, with all her determination, Mrs. Lieu would have been obliged to submit to one or more concubines being installed on her premises.

The limit to these plural wives is a matter of taste or fancy, sometimes of finances, with the master of the house. If he wants heirs (and all Chinese do) and his first and second wives do not bear them, he takes a third, fourth, and so on, at his pleasure. General Li Tsung Tai is reported to have thirteen, and among the number two he imported from Japan. This gentleman travels around the port cities of China, accompanied by two or more of his wives, and lives in high style, stopping at the foreign hotels, giving banquets to foreigners, and consuming champagne, cigars, and cigarettes with the zest of youth, though he is over sixty. His son, Li Wu Yeh, is following his father's good or bad example, and, although only thirty-five, has four times taken unto himself a wife. It is not usual for a mandarin to indulge in a second wife until over forty; indeed, there is some kind of a law against it, but it cannot be iron-clad, as the infringements are too numerous. In a few instances I have attended professionally these Chinese ladies of rank, and always found them modest and retiring,—sometimes so much so that they would not answer the simplest question directly to me, but would reply to their husbands, who would then answer me. Once or twice they would not see me at all, but would thrust their arm out through a silk curtain from an adjoining room, and, resting their dainty wrists on a silk cushion, held by an old woman-attendant, wait until I counted the pulse, and then withdraw the shapely and ring-bedecked hand. When ladies visited my wife I was obliged to seclude myself, and avoid being seen by them, but, as it is perfectly proper to peep, I enjoyed many stolen glances at these fair daughters of the Celestial Empire. Did I say fair? That is a slip of the pen, and entirely incorrect. They are not fair, but usually quite homely. A pretty Chinese woman is exceedingly rare. They have beautiful hands, but not faces; at least, from an American idea of beauty. Their dress, too, to foreign eyes, is anything but becoming. Such outrageous combinations of color! Blue, canary, pink, purple, green, orange, and scarlet can all be worn by a lady in the same costume, and not be considered out of taste. The hair, too, when dressed, will likely contain a large silver pin and two or more large artificial roses of a bright red, with several leaves of green on each stem. I greatly admire the winter costume of the gentlemen and of the officials; the long, flowing robes of satin, lined with fur and rich in embroideries; but the ladies' costumes are too gay and many-colored to suit foreign ideas of taste. Some of the wealthy families take great interest in flowers, and besides having numerous pots of various kinds of roses, palms, and shrubs in their court-yards, will have a garden outside of the city, surrounded by a ten-foot wall, where they raise many varieties of flowering-plants, and also use the garden as an outing or picnic grounds. When these grounds are visited the male and female members of the family go separately, but at the same time to the garden, and, when inside and safe from public gaze, may unite and enjoy a family festival for a brief period.

Sociability does not exist among the upper classes of China as in America or England. They do not have the elegant club-houses, the athletic sporting-houses, the libraries, reading-rooms, nor chess-clubs. They do have a kind of society in the capital cities composed of all the official representatives of a particular province, each province usually having a special building where its sons may meet, called a Hui T'ang; but there is very little of the social element in these societies. They are formed for political purposes, and are frequently at bitter feud with the society from some other province. These societies often give a banquet, it is true, but always with an object. The guests invited are entertained by one or more of the members for the purpose of obtaining their influence with the Governor or some other high personage, with the hope of securing an appointment to office. A dinner given to merely enjoy the pleasure of entertaining one's friends is a rare, if not non-occurring spectacle.

The dishes at these banquets are frequently costly, and always palatable. There is a false impression abroad that Chinese live on all sorts of filthy and, to us, disgusting dishes. While it is true that in the South the lower class may eat cat- and rat-meat, and in the North the same class will eat dog-meat, yet the Chinese gentleman eats nothing that the American gentleman will not eat, though the style of cooking is very different. But is not the French and German cookery also very different from the English and American?

I have been invited to numerous banquets with Chinese gentlemen of rank, and at first, owing to my ignorant prejudices, I wanted to know all the ingredients of a dish, and would taste it very gingerly, usually to the amusement of my host and fellow-guests. But now I am always glad to accept an invitation to a Chinese banquet, knowing I shall have dishes as delicate and palatable as those served by the best French *chef*. One thing in their cookery should be mentioned; that is, their universal use of the "hsiang yu," or sesame-oil. What the olive-oil is to the Frenchman the "hsiang yu," or fragrant-oil, is to the Chinaman. Its taste, at first peculiar, soon becomes pleasant, and to-day I prefer it to either lard or olive-oil in the preparation of food. The poorer people cannot afford this article, and use the cheap substitute of either peanut-oil or bean-oil, which are coarser articles, and of a rank flavor perfectly detestable to a foreign palate. Some of the dishes served at a banquet are " t'ien ya tzu" (specially-fattened ducks, which are browned to perfection, and of a delicious flavor), " feng chi" (salted chickens, tasting somewhat like ham), " huo t'ui" (a delicate ham, cured without saltpetre, and consequently of the appearance and much the taste of veal), " yü ch'ih" (shark-fin, a beautiful dish of amber gelatin, with sauce), " hai li tzu" (devilled oysters, with mushrooms), " t'ang ts'u yü" (sweet sauce fish ; only China can produce this sauce). I might go on indefinitely describing dishes the bare remembrance of which causes the saliva to flow, but I will forbear. Suffice it to say, that for variety and delicacy I prefer a Chinese banquet to that of any nationality I have had the pleasure of partaking.

Although always given for a purpose, the host's manners are those of perfect hospitality. He entreats you to " eat this," " taste that," etc., assuring you it is very good, and with his own ivory chop-sticks, fresh from his mouth, will select an especially dainty bit from the bowl under consideration and deposit it in your little saucer. If only the dishes would be served in a separate little bowl to each individual, instead of a large communistic bowl in the centre, a Chinese feast would be perfect. Wine of several varieties is served during the banquet, but I cannot commend the wine. At the close, instead of finger-bowls, a napkin wrung out of boiling water is presented each guest, and he proceeds to bathe his face, hands, and head before adjourning to the "mu kang" for his pipe of opium or tobacco, as his habit is. Cigarettes, recently introduced into the country, have become very popular. I have often seen a large, corpulent, and pompous mandarin puffing a very small cigarette, and apparently enjoying it hugely. Although cards and chess doubtless originated in China, the upper classes do not indulge much in either pastime. Some of the gentlemen, and occasionally a lady, will play the banjo or guitar; but music (such as it is) is usually the profession of the blind, the actor, or the harlot, and has few votaries among the gentle class.

Descriptions of ceremonies connected with births, marriages, deaths, and funerals are so common in all the books in China that I will not repeat them here. Williams's "Middle Kingdom" and Nevius's "China and the Chinese" give descriptions that cannot be surpassed, and need not be repeated. A Chinaman of the upper class is always dignified, always courteous, always suspicious, and seldom entirely trustworthy. A misrepresentation of facts does not convey to him the idea of dishonor. He has been taught this from his childhood, and to lie skillfully is a part of his education and training.

The middle class consists of the bankers, business men, their clerks, teachers, and well-to-do farmers. There is not nearly the same large middle class as we have in the United States. In this class there is a nearer approach to the home life of civilized nations than in the class above or below it. The wife has more to say in matters pertaining to the family, and, as there is seldom more than one wife, the family relations are smoother. I was acquainted with a Mr. Li Wen Shu, whose family I attended several times, who might be taken as a representative of this class. This gentle-

A Middle Class Family, the Wife having Bound Feet.

man was a teacher by profession, and at the time of my acquaintance with him was engaged in teaching the children of a rich mandarin in the city. He received as salary fifteen dollars a month. Out of this he rented a house of six rooms, on a retired street, for two dollars and a half per month, and supported his wife and four children—two daughters and two sons—on the remainder. They were always well clothed, well fed, and appeared to think they were in very comfortable circumstances. Mrs. Li was a bright, intelligent little woman, of about forty years of age, and had acquired from her husband a fair education, so that she was enabled to teach her sons and daughters.

The seclusion of females, so strictly carried out in the upper class, is relaxed considerably in the middle class, and friends of the family, even chance acquaintances, are often permitted to come into the interior or family living-rooms. The young maidens are, however, expected to go into inner rooms, separated only by a cloth curtain, on such occasions, where they can hear all the conversation, but remain unseen. And this conversation is usually on one topic, namely, money. No matter where you stop to listen to two Chinamen in conversation, the topic will invariably be money and the prices of various commodities. Ch'ien, ch'ien, ch'ien (cash, cash, cash) you hear all around you; your servant, your teacher, your acquaintance, your friends talk of nothing but money. "How much did this cost?" "How much did he pay for that?" How this man made something out of that one, etc., etc. Anecdotes of clever swindles are greatly enjoyed, and a Chinaman having a story of how some mutual acquaintance was fleeced out of the value of five cents to relate is always sure of an attentive audience.

Young single men and maidens are never permitted to mingle, or even meet, in this or any other class of society; consequently, all matches are arranged by middle parties, or go-betweens. Frequently great fraud is practiced in these marriage contracts, and the bride or groom grossly imposed upon.

Many cases of this kind of imposition came under my observation. I will record but two. The first, a woman of twenty-three years of age, came to the dispensary, accompanied by her mother, for the cure of hare-lip. The mother said she had been married over a year, but that the husband had been so angered when he removed the bridal-veil and saw the deformity that he had refused to cohabit with her, but had maintained her in separate apartments, and had taken every opportunity to abuse and revile her. They admitted that the husband had been informed that his intended wife was beautiful and without fault, and the fact of her deformity concealed. They now came to me for an operation, having met a former patient whom I had relieved of this disfigurement. Not having any ether, I asked the young woman if she could stand the pain of an operation. " How long will it last ? " she inquired. " About five minutes," I answered. "Oh, is that all ?" said she; "why, I would stand it two weeks if it would cure my mouth." She sat perfectly still while I performed the necessary operation, including the extraction of a tooth which projected directly to the front, and, when some three months later she accompanied her mother to the dispensary, she told me her husband was very fond of her now and awfully pleased with her " new mouth."

The other case was a Mr. Chiang, a teacher of my acquaintance, a widower. He desired again to enter

Hymen's bonds, as, he stated, he had no one to keep house and mend his shirts for him.   A middle-man informed him that a widow-lady, without children, a Mrs. Chao, who was virtuous, cleanly, and of a good family, but poor, was willing to espouse him.   The contract was made and the ceremony performed, two days after which the lady informed Mr. Chiang that she was dying to see her two children, and would leave him if they were not sent for

Thereupon ensued a scene.   The middle-man was sent for, and, on arriving, fell at Mr. Chiang's feet and humbly begged his pardon, assuring him that the woman was a relative of his whom he would have had to support if he could not secure a husband for her, and wound up by assuring him that the two children, aged fifteen and thirteen respectively, would be an honor to him and grace his old age.   Mr. Chiang at last relaxed, and finally sent for the children, and is bringing them up as his own.   His friends made a great deal of sport of him, which he took very good naturedly, always ending, himself, with the remark, " Yes, I was a great fool, but I had nobody to mend my shirts."

It is by the middle class that all the business of the country is transacted.   The business firms, for the most part, are small concerns; but in the ports there are some very large merchant-houses, whose heads are capable of competing with the firms of foreign houses established for native traffic.   Japan, Siam, Singapore, Australia, and the Hawaiian Islands all contain many business firms composed of Chinese of the middle class, and their honesty and respectability can well compare with firms of any other nationality.   A middle-class farmer is, perhaps, the most independent man in the empire, and if I were a Chinaman I would rather be a farmer in good circumstances than an official.

His neighbors all call him the "ts'ai chu" (rich man), and treat him well; and if not too rich, so as to attract the greed of the officials, he may live happily and unmolested in the village of his forefathers. Such a man is Mr. Li San Wei. At the age of fifty he no longer needs to work himself, for he owns a hundred and fifty "mou" (native acres) of good land, a house of twenty "chien" (rooms) with tile roofs, a horse, a mule, and two donkeys. Besides, he has three sturdy and strong sons to work and one son studying for a teacher. Being the wealthiest man in the village of Ma Chia Chuang, he is consulted upon all matters pertaining to the village, and his opinions received as law. Even the village-teacher is glad to bow to him and call him Hsiensheng. His wants, being simple, are easily supplied at the five-day market, and, in the blest consciousness that, having four sons, his tomb will be properly worshiped, he can live quietly on until, surrounded by his children, he peacefully departs to the spirit-world.

Visiting and social enjoyment, such as are common in Western countries, do not prevail. At times, when a public theatrical entertainment is provided by some benevolent gentleman, the wives of a given neighborhood will decorate themselves and their daughters and ride in company upon wheelbarrows to the place of entertainment, where, seated upon the ground or on chairs carried for the occasion, they will eat peanuts and gossip as only the gentler sex know how. Young women after marriage are usually permitted to make stated visits to their mother, when not too distant; but frequent visiting of any kind is unusual.

There are certain days set apart for mourning, and, on the arrival of one of these days, the women of the household purchase a quantity of paper money, as it is called; being gold and silver paper shaped like the shoes of silver used in exchange. With these they repair to the family burying-ground, and after burning them as an offering to the departed, they, in chorus, lament at the top of their voices. Their lamentation becomes particularly loud and distressing if they are observed, but if they believe no one near they relapse into quiet conversation. After a half-day spent in this pleasant occupation, they return home with the consciousness of having performed a duty.

The laboring class is by long odds the majority of the population. The most of them perform what is called coolie work, which may be said to include farm-laborers, carters, wheelbarrow-men, burden-carriers, letter-runners, muleteers, chair-bearers, boatmen, and any occupation in which the strength and endurance of the man is the chief requisite. A grade above these are the masons, carpenters, blacksmiths, iron-workers, brass-workers, silver-smiths, and tin-smiths, who require higher wages, wear better clothes, and eat better food. A good carpenter will earn from fifteen to seventeen and one-half cents per day wages, while a coolie frequently will obtain but from five to ten cents. I met a group of farm-laborers going to work one day at dawn, while I was *en route* to Wei Hsien, and desired my carter to ask them how much they were paid daily. I knew if I asked them myself I would not get the truth. They replied to him ninety small cash a day and their board. This was near harvest-time, and their ninety small cash is equivalent to four and one-half cents. Each man carried his own implement on his back and, besides, had his long pipe and bag of tobacco. These, with a reed-hat and a pair of blue-cotton pants, completed an outfit.

Vast numbers of these laboring men never marry, and never have any home. They are connected with various hongs or corporations, which give them employment, as the cart-hong, the boat-hong, the wheelbarrow-hong, etc. If not connected with a hong and sent out by it to do special work, they obtain employment when and how they can, often going hungry to sleep on the ground, never having sufficient to be considered comfortably clothed and fed; yet, with a population largely composed of this element, in whom we would naturally expect discontent and rebellion, we find very little of it. As far as I can judge, the Chinese laborer is the most patient, contented man on earth. He thinks his position is inevitable, and, like the philosopher that he is, he quietly endures what he cannot cure. Even in the districts flooded by the Yellow River, where thousands are rendered homeless and have to live until they starve in matsheds upon the river-bank, very little complaint is heard. The professional beggar will cry and whine in a most piteous manner, but the unfortunate laborer will die without murmur when left helpless from lack of employment or illness. Occasionally a carter or other laborer marries and has a home, if it can be called such. It usually consists of one room, or part of a room, in an alley or small street, in which the family live, sleep, and cook, though the cooking is, in fine weather, done just outside the door. As the husband cannot furnish sufficient money to run the family, the wife is obliged to make shoes, sew garments, or perform some labor which will bring in a few cash and help the exchequer. Often the husband is absent from home for a year or more at a time, and the wife is obliged to support herself and children in the meantime. This kind of married life holds out little inducement in the way of happiness, and it is no wonder that most of the men prefer not to encumber themselves with the burden of a family. I have asked many of the wheelbarrow-coolies whether they were married or not, and invariably received an answer in the negative.

The young farmers, with scarcely more to subsist upon than the coolies, usually marry, and as their family increases so does their poverty. It really seems a blessing that the infant mortality is as high as it is, as to nourish and rear all who are born is an impossibility in many families. It is not because food is dear, but because the country is overpopulated and wages consequently exceedingly low. If manufactures, mining, and other avenues of employment were open, the condition of the laborer could not but improve. It is owing to this glut of laborers that so many of the natives of the South have emigrated to the United States, Australia, and Hawaii, in hopes of bettering their condition. The United States has acted in a very unjust manner in discriminating against the Chinese by restrictive immigration laws. They are by far more peaceful, intelligent, and industrious than the Italians or Hungarians, who are dumped in such numbers annually at our Eastern seaports. During the years 1881 and 1882 I resided in the coal-mining district of middle Pennsylvania, and had good opportunities for studying the immigrants from Europe. With the exceptions of the Scotch and the Swedish immigrants, I believe they are all more undesirable than the Chinese. If the people of the United

States believe that pauper immigration is an evil, let them close the doors to all alike, making no distinction between the European and the Asiatic. This kind of legislation would be just, if not generous, and would commend itself to all right-minded people.

CHAPTER VII.

PROSTITUTION is one of the vices that is universal, and exists in China, as in all civilized and uncivilized countries of the globe. The brothels of China are, however, very unlike those of the neighboring country of Japan. In China the inhabitants of brothels are despised and reviled, even by those who cohabit with them; while in Japan the public prostitute does not lose caste, and may, and frequently does, marry to advantage amongst the upper class. You never, in a Chinese city, see a company of young men and prostitutes out on a revel, as is so often the case in Japan.

In riding from Tokio to Yokohama, in the latter kingdom, the past winter, I saw a party of four young men and three quite pretty and gaily-painted prostitutes in the same car, who were having a glorious time. They had two or three bottles of various liquors, oranges, and fancy cakes, and they ate, drank, and sang, besides playing jokes on each other and frolicking like so many kittens. You may travel the whole length of the Chinese Empire and never witness such a scene. A Chinaman's sense of dignity is too great to allow him to unbend in public sufficient to carouse in such an open manner. Even the young scamp who dissipates and visits brothels is correct enough when outside of their walls.

The Chinese prostitute is usually the child of very poor parents, who have been obliged to neglect their children. She first begs, and then is enticed into a

8　　　(113)

life of gilded sin by some designing scoundrel, or by some old woman who is a procuress and earns her living by obtaining recruits for brothels. The unfortunate blind girls, too, are often given away by their parents, who do not care to kill them,—and these poor girls are taught to play musical instruments and sing, and become public prostitutes. In the south of China there are many of these blind prostitutes, but in the North they are not so commonly met with.

A man is not considered disgraced in any way by visiting brothels, or, if he has considerable means, of having prostitutes brought to his house. But if he should become enamored of a prostitute and marry her, he is laughed at by his friends.

A gentleman of my acquaintance, a Judge Kuo, who has been magistrate of the T'ang I and Chi Yang districts since our friendship began, and who was a constant visitor at my house, told me the following story about his cousin, also a Judge Kuo:—

This man, when sixty years of age, was taking a half-ounce of opium daily, by the pipe, and, feeling that if he continued he would lose his public office, became anxious to quit the habit. A Chinese doctor, who had studied with a foreign physician, undertook his cure, and was quite successful; but there was one symptom, occasioned by withdrawal of the narcotic, that this native doctor could not combat, namely, erotic excitement. The old judge had lost his wife ten years before, and had kept no mistress in the meantime, because the opium he used kept his passions in abeyance. Now, however, that the drug was withdrawn, his passions returned with renewed vigor, and he was anxious to indulge in sexual intercourse. The native physician forbade this, and for several nights the old gentleman suffered nocturnal emissions. On the fifth day, word came from the Emperor, from Peking, demanding his immediate attendance at the capital; so, leaving his physician behind, he, with his retainers, some twenty-odd men, took carts and proceeded toward Peking to obey the imperial mandate.

The first night of the journey he stopped at the city of Ch'i Hŏ, but fifteen miles from Chinanfu, and, as soon as he retired, the erotic sensations overcame him. Not having his doctor along to interdict him, he determined to gratify his passions; so, calling his head-servant, he desired him to visit the brothels of the city and procure for him a concubine. This was done, and the old judge was so well pleased with the woman that he carried her along to Peking with him. During the journey she became pregnant, greatly to the joy of the old man, who previously had no issue; and when, in due course of time, she gave birth to a *male* child, the old judge was so completely happy that he married her in proper style, and gave her the title of his lady. She then dismissed all the former retainers of her husband (who, of course, knew her history), hoping to prevent her former estate from being known; but the story leaked out, and, although the old judge continued devoted until his death, a few years later, yet the wife was never received into society, and the judge himself became the laughing-stock of his friends.

This story, which I affirm to be true, upon the word of my friend, Judge Kuo Chun Hsi, proves the essential difference in the attitude of the Chinese, as compared with the Japanese, toward prostitution. While, as a rule, no effort is made to prohibit it, yet it is hidden, or carried on very quietly, and the prostitute is forever condemned as an outcast. On the contrary, in Japan it is practiced openly ; the prostitute is frequently well-educated, refined in manner, and may even become an influential leader of society,—as the wife of a noble or official of rank. It is true, that at times spasmodic efforts to repress prostitution are made by some particularly upright judge in his own district, but these efforts are few and far between, and, usually, the next incumbent of the magistracy will allow all the good his predecessor accomplished fall to the ground.

In the early seventies, a Judge Yuan occupied the magistracy of Chinanfu, who will be long remembered by the people of that district. This judge, although a heathen, or, more correctly speaking, a Confucianist, was a good and just man. As soon as appointed judge, he ordered all gambling-houses and places of prostitution to close their doors, and gave a few days only to the constables to carry the order into effect. When the time had expired, he sent out his police and had all the prostitutes in the city arrested and brought into his yamen-yard. An eye-witness of the scene assured me that the yard, which is by no means a small one, was full. Girls of twelve, up to women of forty and over, some gaily painted and well-dressed, some in rags, many with eyes heavy from large doses of opium,—for nearly all the lost women take to the drug as a dissipation and as a means to relieve pain.

The judge then issued a proclamation declaring the character of the women, and that he hoped to make honest wives of them by selling them off at auction the following day. Any farmer or business man who was unmarried would be allowed to purchase one. No one was allowed to buy more than one. A great crowd attended the sale, some to buy a wife, but most, of course, to witness the proceedings. At the hour named the judge and his chief of police appeared, and, after repeating a declaration of the character of the women, said they would not sell to the highest bidder, as at first proposed, but that each man in the audience desiring to purchase a wife could select his bargain from the many in the yard, and she would be sold by weight. For some time no one would pick out one; but at last an old farmer, who felt time to be precious, walked up and picked out a woman some forty years of age, who was stout and hearty. "Weigh her," said the judge; and immediately, screaming and kicking, she was hoisted in the balance. "Ninety catties," said the weigher. "But how much a catty?" said the old farmer, rather scared lest his money was insufficient. Curiously enough, nothing had been said about the price per catty. The old judge was a shrewd man, and fond of a joke, withal; so he immediately asked, "What is the price of pork to-day?" "Ninety cash a catty," replied the auctioneer. "Then, sell them at ninety cash," ordered the judge. After this the sale waxed fast and furious, and by night the last one was sold off. One young farmer, having bought one of the younger women, seated her on his wheelbarrow and wheeled toward home for a distance of three miles, when his purchase complained of feeling sick, and, on his asking what was the trouble, she told him she was accustomed to using three drachms of opium daily, and that she would die if she did not obtain some speedily. The poor farmer was sadly perplexed, as well as frightened, but immediately wheeled his purchase back to the sale and requested to see the auctioneer.

At first no one would listen to him; but the judge,

who personally superintended the entire day, observing some trouble on the border of the crowd, soon had the man brought before him. " What is the matter, my man ? " he kindly inquired. The poor fellow fell on his knees, and, striking his head in the dust again and again, said, " Your Honor, the woman I bought will ruin me; so I have brought her back." " How ruin you ? " inquired the judge. " Why, she takes three drachms of opium daily, your Honor, and my earnings altogether are not enough to buy her opium," replied the trembling countryman. " Then she won't do for you," said the judge ; " but see if you cannot find one who does not use the drug, and, if you succeed, have her weighed. If she is heavier you pay the difference in weight, and if lighter you will be refunded; how will that do ? " And the judge smiled to see the expression of intense relief visible on the young man's countenance. The delighted farmer hastened to do as told, and secured a woman who professed to be free of the habit, and who was only too glad to leave her former condition to become the wife of an honest farmer. What those did who bought the heavy opium-eaters I have not been able to find out, but I was told that many of the women became good wives to the farmers and small tradesmen who purchased them. Others found the new life too irksome, and sooner or later relapsed into their old habits. I would not for a moment uphold this method of dealing with the social evil, but simply record, without comment, this instance of Oriental justice as given to me by a resident of the city, who was an eye-witness of the sale.

I have stopped at inns for the night when on journeys through the interior, and have seen prostitutes enter and remain in the rooms of guests during the night.

Sometimes separated from them only by a paper partition, I have heard their conversation and singing. Their music is abominable,—a strum of an instrument between a guitar and a banjo, often not in tune, accompanying a screech of the voice too shrill by any stretch of an American imagination to be called music. Occasionally, through an open door-way, I have seen a Chinaman lying at full length on the kang, with his opium-pipe in his mouth, and the little spirit or oil opium-lamp burning dimly on the small table at his head, while the charmer, with cheeks of brilliant carmine, sat by his side strumming and screeching, to his intense satisfaction, if you could judge by the dreamy look of happiness in his little almond optics.

Prostitutes never parade the streets in the cities of the North, nor, in fact, ever leave their quarters except in a closed sedan-chair, to visit the house of some patron; but in the villages, known as the *stages* on the great roads along the line of constant travel, they frequently visit the inns and solicit travelers. If, however, you but speak to the landlord, they will not be allowed to visit your room. Foreigners who cannot speak the language have sometimes had difficulty in getting rid of this class of intruders when once they had obtained entrance. The following incident, one of several that came to my knowledge, was amusing:—

Rev. Mr. A., a missionary, desiring to get out of the city, where he was residing, for change of air, took his teacher, a Mr. Yang, an old Mohammedan, along with him on a cart journey for several weeks. Old Mr. Yang afterward became my teacher, and he used to chuckle greatly in telling this story: " We had stopped," said he, " for the night at the village of Ch'ang Shan, and as our candles were exhausted and the inn-keeper had none, Mr. A. desired me to go out on the street and purchase ome. Just after I left the room Mr. A. walked into the back court to look after the cart-mule, which was a little lame, leaving his door open. He returned in a few moments, and there sat two painted women on his bed, strumming guitars. They smiled and ogled Mr. A., and asked him if he didn't want company. Poor Mr. A. is an extremely modest and sensitive man, and his position must have been very embarrassing. He assured them he did not want company, and desired them to leave. They only smiled sweetly, and one commenced to sing. Mr. A. became desperate; he pictured to himself all the horrible things that would be said of him if some other missionary or traveler should stop at the same inn. It was too awful to think about; so, rising to the emergency, he caught hold of the two women and forced them screaming through the door, which he immediately bolted, and sat down in a cold perspiration in the dark. After a short time he shouted lustily for the inn-keeper from the inside, but the prostitutes, who, after several ineffectual efforts to regain admittance, had informed the landlord that his guest was a 'crazy foreign devil,' had so frightened that worthy that he declined to hear. Just at that juncture I returned," continued Mr. Yang, " and as I passed through the gate with the candles the landlord told me to go at once to 'top side,' for the foreign teacher was shouting wildly, and no one knew what he wanted. I hastened up to the door and knocked, when poor Mr. A. yelled out, ' Go away, you bold, bad women; I told you I did not want you. Oh, gracious! what a terrible position! Why don't Mr. Yang come back !' ' I am here—it's me, Mr. A. ;' and then," wound up the old man, "he pulled me inside, bolted the door, and told me that if I left the inn-yard again, even for a minute, he would go with me."

Although the recruits to the ranks of the prostitutes come largely from the poor, deserted, and blind girls, yet young widows also fall into this life not infrequently. Widows are looked down upon if they re-marry, and if widowed young they have to choose between a life of virtue and abstinence or of gratification and disgrace. Frequently they try to appear virtuous and obtain gratification secretly. But in all such cases the truth is sooner or later known, and, disgraced beyond repair, they leave their families to become public prostitutes. There are not many brothels of the better class, for the official and wealthy men, being able to maintain one or more concubines, do not patronize houses of prostitution to any great extent. But in China there is a large class of laboring men who are enforced celibates, their occupation not being sufficiently remunerative to support a wife, to whom marriage is an utter impossibility. These seek to gratify their sexual instincts at houses or, more properly speaking, hovels of prostitution of the lowest order. Wherever troops are quartered there is sure to be a great deal of license, and disease of venereal origin is, in consequence, rife at all such places. In the prefectural cities, where the triennial examinations are held, there is always a great amount of prostitution, and many young men, coming from the rural districts to obtain their degrees, are enticed into these places and become diseased for life. I have noticed that during the examinations our dispensary records showed more venereal cases than at any other time in the year, or in years when no examinations were held. Drinking and prostitution are evils usually associated, and China cannot be considered an exception to the rule. Indeed, in the port cities the houses of prostitution are in connection with dram-shops; but in the interior, where foreign ideas have not prevailed, it is not so commonly the case. Drinking among the Chinese is not the great evil that it is in America or England.

There is very little drunkenness; possibly this may, to some extent, be due to the unpalatable production of the stills, but I believe the greatest reason is that a drunkard is so looked down upon by every one that the weight of public opinion is the real cause of the prevailing sobriety. True, you occasionally meet a man the worse for liquor; but it is a rare sight, and, unfortunately, occurs oftener where there are foreigners in number and foreign liquors sold than where the native exists uncontaminated, if I may use the word, by foreign influence. The native liquors are of two kinds,—the " shao chiu," or fire wine, and the " huang chiu," or yellow wine, so called from its color and the fact that it is made from the yellow, glutinous millet. The " shao chiu" in the North is a distilled liquor made from the berry of the broom-corn, or "kao liang," and is an impure alcohol containing much fusel-oil, having a specific gravity varying from 940 to 890, depending largely upon the honesty of the dealer. The people of China nearly all drink wine at feasts and upon great occasions, and among wealthy families and officials it is used with every meal; but the size of the wine-cups makes it obvious that they do not drink to become intoxicated, for when drinking the " shao chiu," the alcoholic strength of which is about equivalent to good brandy, the wine-cup will only hold two drachms, and in drinking the " huang chiu," or millet-wine, the cup contains but an ounce of a wine equal in alcoholic strength to ordinary claret. This millet-wine is made in all the cities of the North, and is a very variable product, both in regard to taste and alcoholic strength. In some places I have found it to be exceedingly pleasant, and very like a light-brown sherry; in other places, of a very dark brown, and of a smoky, disagreeable taste, that was very uninviting. All wines are drank hot, and many of the natives consider cold wine as next to poison.

The effect of drinking the "shao chiu" is very apparent, in those who habitually use it, in several ways. There is always constipation, more or less gastric catarrh, and frequently a stricture of the œsophagus. Of this latter trouble I shall speak in another place. There can be no doubt that the ingestion of even small quantities of this liquor, rich as it is in fusel-oil, cannot but be injurious both locally and constitutionally. The "huang chiu," as far as I have observed, is a harmless and, perhaps, useful beverage. Its percentage of alcohol is low, and being usually but a fermentation of the glutinous millet, with the addition of a small quantity of sugar, it is to the Chinese what claret is to the French and beer to the Germans, only it is not near so universally used; for although costing, on an average, but six to eight cents a pint, yet even this small sum places it as a luxury, to the ordinary working-man, reserved for feast days and great occasions.

There are many varieties of these two liquors. Some steeped with leaves of certain flowers and named therefrom are highly esteemed; others with spices, such as cinnamon, which is supposed to be especially good in averting the consequences of taking cold. But, whatever the name, the liquor is essentially either a "shao chiu" or a " huang chiu," and may be so classed. The use of grapes, of which they have several varieties, in making wine is an idea which has not yet occurred to John Chinaman; but we may be sure that in the next few years the foreigner who brings him things good, bad, and indifferent will give him a knowledge of wine-making from the grape, and we may confidently expect clarets and burgundies of Chinese manufacture that will undersell the products of the California vineyards.

Wine has not been, so far, to China the curse it has been in Europe and America, but in opium she has a curse more potent and terrible in ruining and degrading her people than even King Alcohol. The history of how opium was introduced into China—nay, forced upon the country—by the British is a matter of history, and needs no repetition here. Suffice it to say that many of the best subjects of the British Empire, realizing the disgrace attaching to their country from the opium traffic forced upon China in the first place, and maintained even now against the Chinese inclination, are at present endeavoring to rouse the people of their country to move Parliament in favor of the total abolition of the opium traffic. But, even if they succeed, they cannot undo the evil entirely, for the Chinese, having become used to the enticing drug, are now raising it in no small quantities in their own country. Although there are severe penalties attached to the raising of the poppy, and each magistrate is obliged to report to the Governor that none is grown in his district, yet I have seen it grown in large patches right alongside of the great road on the main lines of traffic; and when questioning the farmers as to how they dared do this, in open defiance of the law, they would grin, and reply, " Our judge will smoke some of

The Hall of the Classics at Peking

this, and he won't dare tell who smokes the rest." In some of the provinces much more is smoked than in others; that is, the smoking is more universal. In the province of Shan Hsi I am told that in a number of the villages men, women, and children all use the pernicious drug, and that on entering such a village you can tell at a glance, by the dilapidated condition of all the houses, temples, etc., that the entire village is composed of opium debauchees.

Nearly every village in Shantung has its opium-shop, and it is sold at all the fairs and market-places. The wealthy or official classes are, however, the heaviest indulgers. I have frequently been in the houses of wealthy men of high rank, when a friend would enter, and, after the usual greetings and salutations, would be invited to recline on the "mu kang," or carpeted platform, and partake of a pipe or two of opium. I well recall a scene I witnessed two years ago. I was daily visiting a Judge Hŏ, a wealthy ex-magistrate, who was slowly dying of Bright's disease. He daily consumed two ounces of the drug, and yet stated he was taking less at this time than formerly. On the day I speak of he was sitting on a raised platform, reclining against the chest of a servant, whom he would not allow to move from his position. He assured me he felt more comfortable leaning against this man than against a chair-back, although he had purchased several expensive chairs to try.

Dressed in a crimson-silk gown, lined with white Siberian fox-skin, this poor, emaciated skeleton would entertain his friends in royal style, laughing and joking with them, and apparently taking as much interest in all that was going on about town as though he were in good health, or could ever expect to be. A little maiden dressed in scarlet silk, with many-colored trimming, called "lan kan," sat at his knee and filled and refilled his water-pipe, lighting it and placing it in his mouth for one puff, then extinguishing and reloading as before. I sat in front of him, and, having felt his pulse and looked at his tongue, was preparing a prescription, when a bustle was heard in the yard and a servant appeared, and, having saluted, presented a card and said: "The great General P'an, his Majesty's commissioner for the military examinations, is without, and desires to pay his respects to you." "Invite him in," said the judge. "Don't go, Doctor," he continued; "General P'an is an old friend of mine, and I desire you to meet him."

He had no sooner finished than the general was introduced, and the two friends saluted in the usual fashion, except that Judge Hŏ, being unable to stand upon his dropsical legs, bowed and shook his own hands. "Allow me to introduce to you, General, my friend, the great Dr. Coltman, whose skill the whole city knows, and who has come thousands of miles to alleviate the diseases of our flowery land." I bowed low to the distinguished general, and said: "Our friend, Judge Ho, is too good, and I dare not take the honors he would heap upon me." "You are too modest," replied the general; "what he says is true, and I am glad to meet you. What is your honorable country?" "My poor, miserable native land is America," I replied. "Oh, you come from the great, beautiful land where everybody is rich. Much I would like to visit your land, of which I have heard so much; but I am eighty years old now, and fear the sea."

Then followed a few questions and answers, and the general accepted an invitation to recline upon the "mu kang" and take a pipe of opium. He was no sooner comfortably fixed than a Judge Ch'en, who had been broken the bench for some offense, but had recently been pardoned, and was now about to start to Peking to visit the Emperor before again taking office, dropped in to say good-bye, and, on being invited, also took his place upon the "mu kang" for a pipe. Then Magistrates Kung and Kuo—the one the brother-in-law, the other the life-time friend of old Mr. Hŏ—dropped in, and the conversation became very animated. These gentlemen would talk awhile, and then recline on the "mu kang" to smoke a pipe or two.

Refreshments and tea were served from time to time, and I was not allowed to depart for over an hour. Old Judge Hŏ would doze off from time to time, but every once in awhile would rouse up and ask some question, or reply to something said, even though he appeared to be sleeping. The old general, eighty years of age, said in answer to my question that he had only been taking opium the last ten years, and did not use above a drachm or two a day, which he merely took for sociability and to please his friends. His general appearance was that of perfect health, and he said he ate well and slept well, his only trouble being a constipated condition of his bowels. Messrs. Kung and Kuo consumed, respectively, two and three drachms daily of the drug.

I should say a large majority of the officials or mandarins use opium to greater or less extent, some only using a drachm or less daily, while many consume two ounces or more. Those who use such large amounts soon become helplessly besotted, and are unfit for any active duty. The wives of many of these men also use greater or less quantity of it, and show in their wasted, yellow faces and sunken, hollow eyes the evil effects of the dissipation. I have noticed the bad effects of opium upon those who had to undergo a surgical operation, as have also many of my professional brethren in China; and I was quite surprised to see a paper written by the colonial surgeon at Hong Kong Hospital and Jail, stating that a man placed in jail and deprived of all opium suffered no evil effects therefrom, and that the opium-eaters bore operations as well, even when deprived of the drug, as others. The explanation of this, to my mind, lies in the fact that the gentleman who put such a statement into print is the hired servant of her British Majesty's administration, and allows policy to take the place of truth.

An evil which has sprung up from the opium habit is the manufacture and sale of pills advertised to cure the habit, but containing as their chief ingredient a variable amount of morphia. Many are cured of the pipe and take pills instead, which is much the more pernicious habit, having a more direct and damaging effect upon the alimentary tract. A number of times I have asked people, " Do you take opium?" and they replied, "Oh, no ; I used to, but I don't any more. I take pills now." "Can you stop taking the pills?" " Oh, no." " Then, are you any better off with the pills than with the pipe?" " Yes, a great deal, because the pills do not require the time that the pipe used to, and do not interfere with my occupation."

There are many opium refuges established by the various missionary societies in different places, and, although there are, undoubtedly, numbers who relapse into their former bad habits after having been cured at these places, yet the results, on the whole, appear to be very satisfactory, and worthy of continuance as a form of missionary and philanthropic effort.

The methods pursued in the cure at the refuges are known as the total withdrawal and the gradual withdrawal plans. Each plan has its warm advocates. I have tried both plans in patients under my care, and have come to believe that some patients who would die if suddenly deprived of the drug can be cured by its gradual withdrawal, while others who are robust and not taking too heavy a daily dose can be best treated by an entire withdrawal of the opium. Strychnia, quinia, capsicum, caffeine, gentian, and preparations of iron are all used as part of the treatment. Many have found strong infusions of black coffee, with or without a little brandy, to be valuable. Vomiting, purging, and other symptoms, as they arise, to be treated by the appropriate remedies. Should symptoms of collapse be observed, all agree that there is nothing so available as a hypodermatic injection of morphia.

The older the patient, the less likelihood of his persisting in a cure. I attended one old gentleman, sixty-two years of age, who said he was willing to undergo anything to be cured of the habit. He took three drachms daily. He stood reduction by the gradual plan very well, until he was taking but a drachm daily; but, at this point, he declined to be treated further, and said his family were afraid for him to give it up entirely. Although I urged him strongly to continue treatment and be cured, he would not heed my advice. Three months later he was taking a drachm and a half, and doubtless by this time is back to his former allowance, and, of course, in time, will exceed even that.

Occasionally I have met an individual who assured me he had been taking from half a drachm to a drachm, by the pipe, for ten years, and had not increased it at all in that time. I have always doubted such statements, though I cannot affirm such a thing to be impossible; for, whereas the usual tendency is certainly to gradually increase the daily amount, still, as some in America use liquors constantly without increasing the amount consumed, may not some of the Chinese take opium in the same way?

As to tobacco-smoking, it is universal. Everybody smokes, but the pipes are usually very small, and do not hold more than enough for half-a-dozen puffs at one loading. They are all made with brass bowls, with a long reed stem and a brass or stone mouth-piece. Some of these mouth-pieces are curiously carved and are quite expensive. The tobacco smoked is a native product and poor in nicotine; so that very little, if any, harm can be done by this habit. There is a strong tobacco raised in Manchuria, and sold in the northern provinces, that is very rich in nicotine, and would make good cigars; but the price of this article is so much more than the home product, that the majority of the Chinese cannot afford it. There are a few of the Chinese who do not smoke do not drink, do not smoke opium, and do not, according to their statements, do anything bad. They are not safe to have around.

CHAPTER VIII.

DISEASES PREVALENT IN CHINA.

ANY one reading the hospital and dispensary reports from all over China, will be at once struck by the unanimity with which all observers class diseases of alimentation as the most frequently met with. Dyspepsia of various forms takes precedence in all these reports. Why is this so? The people are an active race (that is, the male portion of the community; for, in the North, where foot-binding is universal, the females are unable to take much exercise on their deformed little feet), and we are told digestion depends to considerable extent upon proper exercise. But it also depends upon the ingestion of properly cooked, nutritious food, that is easily assimilated. Now, the diet of the majority in the North is anything else.

The upper class can obtain whatever they desire, and usually live well. The middle class can enjoy a sufficiency of proper food, of a digestible nature, also; but by far the largest class of China is the laboring class, who barely earn enough to secure food of the coarsest description, containing so little aliment that a large quantity has to be ingested to support life. This results in dilatation of the stomach and thinning of its walls, with consequent impairment of its function. Millet and " kao liang " (the berry of the broom-corn) are the two chief articles of food, with cabbage, beans, radishes, and cucumbers to help out. Meat is too expensive and can only be indulged in on rare occasions, and even then very sparingly, for a pound of pork at nine cents

(131)

is equivalent to two days' pay of many of the coolies. Then, too, what miserable food they can obtain is hastily cooked, because fuel is so expensive that to properly cook the food would make it too dear; therefore, it is put in the pot, slightly boiled, and then ingested. The infant mortality in China, due to improper feeding, were it known, would astonish the world. This applies to all classes, for the better-off portion of the population lose as many of their offspring from injudicious, improper feeding as the poorer do because of necessity their diet is improper.

Another factor in the production of this class of diseases is the contamination of the water-supply. No attention is paid to hygiene. In a country where the soil is as porous as a sieve, a manure-deposit will be right alongside of a well where the water is but eight or ten feet from the surface, and where the water, on being slightly warmed or stale, emits an odor decidedly fæcal. The Chinese know nothing of the germ-theory of disease, but they know by experience that no water but boiling water is safe to drink. They will look with horror at a foreigner drinking a glass of cold water, and after having several severe illnesses in my own family from drinking what I considered ordinarily pure water, I have adopted the plan of drinking nothing but boiled water, tea, and coffee.

The climate, too, has its influence. The country, as far as explored, has proved malarious, and malaria is certain agent to derange the digestive system. Thus we find that the great prevalence of dyspeptic trouble may be said to be due to three principal causes: improper and badly cooked food, vitiated water, an malarial climate.

Next in frequency to diseases of the alimentary tract are eye troubles. Conjunctivitis, entropion, cataract, keratitis, pannus, granular lids, and trichiases abound. Ulcers of the cornea, with perforation and staphyloma, are very common ; many an eye being lost that, by judicious treatment, could have been saved. Near-sighted people are frequently met with, and the sale of eye-glasses in the future will be a paying business to some enterprising optician.

Pterygium is very frequent, often double, and sometimes triple in both eyes. Glaucoma is very infrequent. Diseases of the kidneys are quite common, but, as post-mortem examinations are, so far, impossible, we cannot say the special form of degeneration. Chronic nephritis coming on gradually is what we meet with usually, having albuminuria, tube-casts, and dropsy as the prominent symptoms. As it is impossible, in most cases, owing to poverty, to place patients upon a proper diet, the progress of the case is downward. Diabetes is occasionally seen. Diseases of the lungs vary very much with location. Along the coast in the North they are frequent, especially asthma and chronic bronchitis. Also in low, damp regions in the interior ; but in some counties in the interior, especially around Wei Hsien, serious lung troubles are scarcely heard of. I have seen a few cases of rapid pulmonary tuberculosis in which the patients, who had previously been in good health, would have a hæmorrhage, usually not severe, followed by high fever, rapid emaciation, and death in from one to two months, before any marked destruction of lung-tissue had taken place. These cases are hopeless from the start. I have tried numerous remedies without the slightest effect in arresting the disease. Men and women seem to be equally affected. In women there is a suppression of menstruation previous to appearance of the hæmorrhage.

Pleurisy occurs frequently, especially during the spring, along the coast-line, but is uncommon in the interior. There is a disease of the spleen characterized by gradual enlargement and hardening of that organ, attended at first by no symptoms other than the increase in size of the abdomen, but gradually the face becomes pale, then the mucous membranes lose all color, the child (for usually it is children who are affected) emaciates, becomes feverish in the evening, and finally dies, either in convulsions or by heart-failure. The blood, on examination by microscope, shows excessive development of white corpuscles and decrease, amounting in some cases to almost absence, of red corpuscles. These cases sometimes do and sometimes do not reside in malarial districts, or have history of previous malarial fever. But all progressively get worse and die, the duration of a case from commencement to the fatal termination being from six months to two years. In some cases the enlargement of the spleen is enormous, distending the abdomen and making pressure upon its viscera; in other cases, while the enlargement is marked, the case goes on to its fatal termination without the spleen interfering by its size with the abdominal viscera. Treatment by hypodermatic injections of ergot, inunction of red iodide of mercury, arsenic, iron, mineral and vegetable alteratives, have all proved futile in my hands, and, as far as I know, in the hands of all other observers. I know of no single case of this disease (leucocythemia) being cured; post-mortems are impossible.

Stricture of the œsophagus is far from uncommon. Some say it is due to the irritative effects of the wine drunk hot, though some of the patients do not drink wine. Others say it is due to syphilis; and this, I think, more likely, as nearly all my cases have improved under dilatation and iodide of potassium administered internally; some under mercury and iodide alone, without dilatation. The native faculty consider this a fatal disease, and call it the starvation disease. One case of this disorder was so advanced when brought to me, and recovered so promptly, that I cannot refrain reporting it. The patient, a man aged forty-two, was brought to the hospital on a stretcher, unable to stand; had not retained food or drink for six days, owing to a stricture of the œsophagus near the cardiac orifice of the stomach; had been troubled over a year with difficulty in swallowing. Upon my giving him a cup of tea he swallowed a mouthful, and it passed down the pharynx, but was immediately after regurgitated into his mouth. I then passed a tolerably firm stomach-pump tube with some difficulty through the constriction and into the stomach; then attached the pump and pumped in a quart of warm condensed milk containing fifteen grains of potassium iodide. Upon withdrawing the tube a great quantity of ropy, tenacious mucus was expectorated. I followed this treatment for ten days three times daily, with the result that at the end of that time he could swallow with some difficulty; stopped using the tube, but continued giving iodide of potassium with a small quantity of bichloride of mercury for twenty days longer, at the end of which time he could swallow even solid food without difficulty, and had gained largely in flesh. Then I dismissed him, with a supply of medicine to last thirty days, and directed him to return if he had any symptoms of a relapse. Two years have passed, and he has not returned; so I think he may be considered cured.

Skin diseases are frequent, and, doubtless, the prevalent filth has a large place as a causative element. The affections most frequently met with are psoriasis, eczema, and the syphiloderm. Herpes zoster is found all over China, too, although this is a neuritis rather than a true skin disease. These diseases, I have found, yield to treatment much more readily than in the United States. Why, I cannot say, unless it is in the almost entire absence of meat from the diet and the employment of vegetable in place of animal oils in the cookery. I say this because I have noticed, in some rather intractable cases, that the patients were of the better class and used more or less meat and fatty oils in cookery.

Chronic ulcerations of the legs, sometimes of frightful extent, are often met with, generally in debilitated and run-down subjects living on an insufficient diet. In regard to the fevers of China, I think the paper prepared by me and read by Dr. Hodge before the Shanghai Medical Conference, in 1890, will give all the desired information. It is as follows:—

On receiving notice of my appointment to prepare a paper under the above title, to read before the Medical Missionary Association of China, I proceeded to write to all my professional brethren in China, with a view to obtaining their experiences; and the collection of facts which I lay before you has been gathered from their replies, hospital reports, and my own experience. I find the field to be investigated a large one, and that apparently but little personal investigation has so far been made. This is due to several reasons: 1. The comparatively recent advent of foreign physicians in China, for, although since Dr. Parker's time there have been a few physicians scattered about at the sea-ports, yet it is only during the past few years that they are penetrating to the interior, and that medical missionaries are beginning to be in a position to make extended observations of the climate and diseases of this land. 2. Want of confidence on the part of the natives to submit for any lengthened period to the treatment of a foreign physician, or, in fact, to any one physician, their rule being to change physicians twice or thrice daily in serious cases if they can afford it. 3. Lack of hospital facilities in many places where fevers might be studied. 4. Impossibility of obtaining post-mortem examinations.

I understood my appointment to mean, what are the fevers of China now, and how they differ, if at all, from fevers of other countries. It is just possible that some of the diseases, to be enumerated, have been introduced from foreign countries; but in the state of the native medical faculty we can get no reliable information, and I fear some of these points, on which information would be desirable and interesting, will never be forthcoming.

I find that variola, or small-pox, is the most common disease of China. By this I mean that nearly every one has it at some period of his or her life, usually in childhood. No region is free from it; it may be called resident everywhere; and epidemics are few, for the reason that the entire adult population have had the disease in childhood. Occasionally you meet with more than usual of it among the children; especially is this so when floods or famines drive people away from their homes and cause them to crowd together, but it is confined to the children. I venture to say that in every Chinese city of size there are always a number of cases of small-pox. Last spring it was worse than usual in Chinanfu, and my wife and three children were all taken ill with it; but all recovered, while a native child on my place, treated by native physicians, changed thrice daily, succumbed. Vaccination is practiced, but the virus is in many cases impure from carelessness in obtaining and from ignorance. I do not doubt that syphilis, scrofula, and tuberculosis are often communicated in this way. Until China has a large body of practical, well-educated native medical men, to whom, as Boards of Health, the hygiene of her cities can be trusted, small-pox, as well as all contagious and miasmatic diseases, must continue to annually decimate her population.

Measles exist here, and about Tĕng Chow Fu appear to be very frequent ; reports from other places also prove their existence in other cities and towns. I have personally seen two well-marked cases occurring in Chinanfu in foreign children, both of whom were born here and had never been away; so that the infection was doubtless from native source. This disease, as nearly as I can discover, is in no way different from our descriptions of it in Western works on practice of medicine, though apparently milder.

Scarlet fever undoubtedly occurs among the natives. I myself have seen but one case of this disease in China, and that occurred in a child four years of age, the daughter of an English missionary. She had ulcerated throat, rose-rash all over the body, high temperature, desquamative nephritis, purulent otorrhœa, and, finally, pneumonia and death. This child had been residing inland for ten months, and I judge the infection must have come from native source.

But other observers have met the disease in native patients, as dispensary reports from Moukden and Peking show. My correspondents also from Shanghai, P'ang

Chuang, and Tientsin report having treated native patients with this disease. Indeed, one of my Tientsin correspondents reports it epidemic there every winter. Observers in other places report having met cases of nephritis who came with a history of a previous fever much resembling scarlatina; while from Canton, Tĕng Chow Fu, Ch'ing Chow Fu, Wei Hsien, and Chefoo, my correspondents have reported that, so far, they had never seen a case. My own opinion is that it is more prevalent in North than in South China, and that possibly it has been introduced by foreigners from England or America. I also believe the temperature of a fairly cool climate to be more favorable to its development than a warmer region.

Erysipelas is very rare in China, but has been reported from Foochow and Soochow, as I glean from hospital reports. Unfortunately, I cannot say whether of idiopathic or traumatic origin. I have met with a few cases myself of traumatic origin, which yielded readily to tincture ferri chloridi. More information on this subject would be valuable, and I hope that any of my brethren having surgical cases followed by erysipelas will promptly report them through our journal.

Typhoid of undoubted type, that is to say, genuine enteric fever, has been reported from Shanghai, Canton, Hainan, Hang Chow, Wei Hsien, Tientsin, and Tĕng Chow Fu, and I myself have met it in this city. It appears to be rather infrequent, as some observers report not having met it, and no one observer has had any large number of cases. But this is one of the diseases that usually requires eight to twelve days to establish a perfect diagnosis, and, consequently, the foreign physician is not retained long enough to decide positively the nature of the case. I believe, when greater confidence is shown in the foreign physician, and more accurate reports are possible, that this disease will be found more common among the natives than is now supposed. Universal testimony to the value of the mineral-acid plan of treatment for this disease lies before me, though in the selection of the acid there is some disagreement, the sulphuric and nitro-muriatic each having their friends. I myself have used both acids, but prefer the latter, especially in those cases complicated by malaria. It is here, perhaps, that I should speak of the so-called typho-malarial fever, and I feel I can do no better than to quote Professor Roberts Bartholow: "By this term is meant typhoid fever complicated with a malarial element. In consequence of the existence of a malarial infection, the symptomatology of typhoid fever is modified, the chief variation from the usual thermal line consisting in the greater excursions of the daily temperature. This modification of the fever has long been known by all well-informed physicians practicing in malarious regions. Dr. Woodward, of the U. S. Army, gave to this combination the name typho-malarial fever, he at first supposing that there was something distinctive in this form of fever, and that its morbid anatomy differed in important particulars from that of typhoid. However, in a paper read before the International Medical Congress at Philadelphia, Dr. Woodward retracted his original observations, and admitted that he had been misled, and that the morbid anatomy of typho-malarial fever is merely that of typhoid. Typho-malarial fever, then, has no reason to be admitted into nomenclature—does not, in fact, exist. All that can be claimed for it is that, when typhoid fever occurs in an individual saturated with malaria, the fever is modified somewhat in its course, has more of the remittent type, and is apt to be protracted, owing to the occurrence of intermittence during convalescence."

If the pathological lesions of the so-called typho-malarial fevers are but the lesions of typhoid, then the term, if used at all, should be distinctly understood to mean typhoid fever occurring in an individual previously subjected to the malarial poison.

Typhus fever is frequently met with all over North China, and as far south as Shanghai, after which it is seldom or never seen.

In 1878 an epidemic occurred in Peking, with heavy mortality rate. In 1886 an epidemic occurred in Shansi. In the spring and summer of 1889 an epidemic occurred in Shantung. It is also reported from Moukden, Peking, Tientsin, T'ai Yuen Fu, Shanghai, Chefoo, Těng Chow Fu, and other places. Its existence has been denied in Canton.

Relapsing fever in China, as in other countries, is found constantly associated with typhus. I saw a number of cases last spring during the epidemic of typhus. It is mentioned as the most common variety of fever at Těng Chow Fu.

Dengue is reported as having occurred in foreigners at Canton, but as that is the only place, and there is no evidence that a native has ever had it, it cannot as yet be classed under our title.

Cholera occurs as an epidemic every few years, and is frightfully fatal. The ports seem to be affected most, but in the summer of 1888 a widespread epidemic swept through Shantung and Chihli from east to west, sweeping away thousands of lives. I believe it has existed in

Chefoo the past five years, as there are perennial out-breaks of it among the natives there. The natives dread this disease very much, and, on being seized with a diar-rhœa during a cholera visitation, immediately give them-selves up for lost, and doubtless many perish from fright alone. I had one case in which all my persuasion could not induce my patient to believe he had not the cholera. Finally, by joking with him, and telling him if he really had it he would not be willing to admit it, I got him in a more hopeful frame of mind, and he soon recovered from his diarrhœa.

Diphtheria is reported from Tientsin, Peking, Chi-nanfu, P'ang Chuang, and Ch'ing Chow Fu. I have seen a number of cases in foreigners and natives in this city, but I get no reports of its existing south of Shan-tung. It is severe and frequently fatal in the natives, though apparently less so in foreigners. This may be due to earlier and more energetic treatment on the part of the foreigners.

Cerebro-spinal meningitis I believe to exist in China, as my own child suffered a well-marked case of it three years since. But I have received no reports of any one else having met it. Bartholow says it has never been reported from Asia.

Whooping-cough is reported as occurring occasion-ally in Tientsin. I have not heard of it elsewhere, and have not personally met a case. I infer that if it exists it is rare.

Rheumatic fever is reported from Foochow as very prevalent. Shanghai, Soochow, Chefoo, Lao Ling, and Hang Ch'ow also report its prevalence. I have seen but one case in four years and a half, and that occurred in a Catholic priest, a native of France. Chronic muscular rheumatism is common all over China, but is unattended by fever.

And now we come to malarial fevers, and I find they are reported from everywhere. From Peking in the North to Canton in the South, every one says they are common. It is interesting, however, to note the different forms the poison manifests in different localities. Thus, I find the intermittent of tertian type to be most common in Peking, Chinanfu, and Wei Hsien.

Quartan intermittent in Korea, Soochow, Foochow, Swatow, Shanghai, and Hangchow.

Remittent is reported as the prevailing type at Chefoo and Tientsin, though intermittents are far from rare. Here in Chinanfu I have never seen a case of quartan ague; it is all intermittent of the tertian or quotidian type.

Since the Yellow River has flooded this region there has been a marked increase in the number of fever cases treated at our dispensary.

Shanghai reports a pernicious type of remittent fever, with scarcely any remission, that is largely fatal.

In answer to my question, How do you treat malarial fevers? I have received about the same reply from all sources. Quinia or some other alkaloids from the cinchona-bark are the specifics. Some prefer quinia sulph., some cinchonidia sulph., others still different alkaloids; but it is universally recognized that Peruvian bark is the specific for malarial poison. Scarcely any have tried the carbolic acid and iodine treatment, which is so popular in Camden, U. S. A., where malaria is especially rife; though from Hangchow we learn that its employment in that vicinity as a prophylactic has been successful. Arsenic is recognized as valuable in the chronic forms.

It has up to the present time been found impractica-
ble, owing to the ignorance and prejudice of the Chinese,
to hold post-mortem examinations, and until that can be
done the pathological appearances and morbid anatomy
of these and perhaps other unrecognized diseases must
remain a secret. But we may fairly conclude that, where
the symptoms so nearly coincide with descriptions in
our works on practice, the morbid conditions producing
them will also coincide, and our treatment, based thereon,
give the desired result. I find, in all the diseases I have
mentioned, that our English and American descriptions
are as perfect for China as for the home lands. To sum
up, then, I believe that, with the exception of dengue
and yellow fever, you will find in China all the fevers
recorded in any American work on practice, and that the
fevers are essentially the same in this land as in America.

Diseases of the alimentary canal other than dyspepsia,
though often dependent upon it, are all to be found, and
none more common than parasites. Nearly every one
has worms. Usually it is the long round-worm which
gives so much belly-ache, sometimes the thread-worms,
and in and around Peking numerous cases of tape-worm
are found, though in six years' residence in Shantung I
never met with a single case of this latter affection.
Santonine lozenges, called " yang t'ang" and " foreign
candy-medicine," are in great demand, and at first were
largely successful; but some unscrupulous manufacturers
have nearly excluded the active constituent from these
lozenges in order to make more profit, and the remedy is
falling into bad repute through their dishonesty. Diar-
rhœas, both acute and chronic, cause a large mortality,
especially amongst the infant population and amongst

foreign residents who have not learned how to live in China; but no one disease carries off as many foreigners annually as dysentery. The following paper on this disease was written last autumn, and published by the author in the *Chinese Medical Missionary Journal*:—

September is pre-eminently the month for this disorder throughout the Shantung province. Some cases make their appearance after the middle of August, but they are only the early birds who tell of the coming flock. In 1890 we had a very severe rainy season, which ended about the 22d of August, and immediately thereafter dysenteries became common. I can make out three distinct forms, which, on account of the character of the stools, I shall class as the gelatinous, gelatino-sanguineous, and the sanguineous. These three are all one disease, and may progress from one form to the other in order named, or may be aborted in either of the first two stages. The gelatinous form is usually attended with very little pain, but more or less straining. It is especially characterized by large amount of the jelly-like material in the stools, resembling perfectly boiled sago; beyond this the stool generally contains more or less of partially or entirely undigested food. Little or no fever, but patients emaciate rapidly and soon have to go to bed. This form is frequently obstinate and hard to deal with, especially prone to attack children and young people under twenty, is always associated with weak stomachic digestion, and often complicated with attacks of vomiting. It may continue as it commenced until cured, or may go on into the second form or stage of the gelatino-sanguineous form. This second form, if it be a continuous process of the first, is characterized by the stools gradually having more or less blood mixed with them, and the addition

10

of pain, griping, and fever to the symptoms already existing. This form, more common and easier treated of the three, will frequently yield to two or three days' treatment; sometimes, however, when severe, and amount of blood in discharges is considerable, it may require some week or ten days to effect a cure. Last form, or sanguineous, is always a continuation of the second form. It is characterized by disappearance entirely or for the most part of the jelly-like material, and the presence of liquid or clotted blood and of well-digested fæces, either fluid or solid. It betokens that the surface degeneration of the mucous membrane of the bowel has largely healed, but that one or more ulcers are in an inflammatory state, and instead of spreading on the surface of the bowel are corroding into it and opening small or large vessels, as the case may be. Pain is now referred to one or more definite localities, and the case is really one of ulcer of the bowel. The hæmorrhage may be severe and exhausting, and clots of size of hen-eggs be passed. These ulcers, if of size, may by their cicatrization so contract the calibre of the bowel as to lead to serious interference with the function of the tube if cured, or they may perforate and produce general peritonitis and death.

The degree of fever in this last form is in definite ratio to the amount of ulcerative process; so that high temperature may be taken as a proof that deep ulcerative action is going on, with perforation as a probable result. As I have treated one hundred and sixty cases of this disease in the past year, and have used a variety of methods, I shall give what I find to be the best plans for each kind as I have classed them. The first variety do best without any opium, and I find the following prescription usually efficacious:—

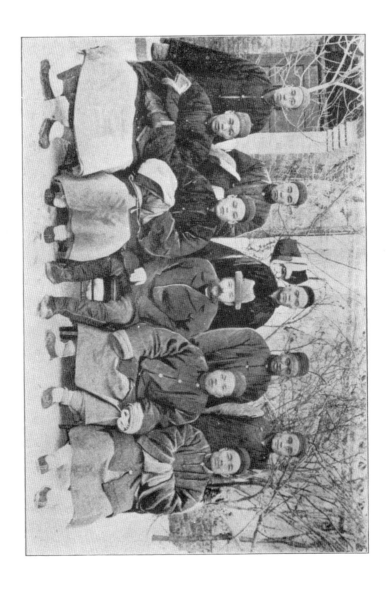

Students of the Têng Chow Fu College.

R Hydrarg. chlor. corrosiv., . . gr. j.
Tr. zingiberis, ... gtt. clx.
Vin. ipecac., ... gtt. lxiv.
Vini spts. rect., ... f℥j.
Sacchar. alb., ... ℥j.
Aqua pura, . . q. s. ft. Oj.

Dose: Teaspoonful every two hours for a
child two or three years old.

Bismuth and pepsin can sometimes be advantageously alternated with this mixture for a few days at a time. If vomiting be an awkward complication it may be usually checked by half-drop doses of carbolic acid in a few drops of glycerin, or by nitrate of silver in doses of one-sixteenth to one-fourth grain in pill. Tinct. cardamom. comp. is useful as a stomachic. Enemas are of no use; the disease in this form is always located near the ileo-cæcal valve, and too high to reach by enemas. Some few cases have seemed to do well under the vegetable astringents, as catechu, kino, etc., but, for the most part, I have found them very unreliable. No matter what the form, I find the time-honored plan of a dose of oil at the beginning very useful, but prefer, to this, drachm doses of Epsom salt given every hour until purgation commences. Diet to consist of soft-boiled rice, eggs, and raw beef or beef-broth and milk; good beef beaten to a pulp in a mortar or shredded finely is a most valuable nutriment, and usually easily digested and assimilated. Care must be taken to avoid chills at night, and little ones should wear a flannel band around the abdomen, which should be changed every twenty-four hours.

In the second form enemas are very useful, and I have found one ounce of tincture of krameria to eight ounces of starch-emulsion, with or without a little laudanum, give the best results,—given three times daily from a fountain syringe.

A pill of pulv. opii, gr. j ; pulv. plumbi acet., gr. iss, every three or four hours, is, in my experience, the best remedy in most instances for the internal treatment. I find also that nearly every case has been benefited by pulverized cinchona-bark, in five- to ten- grain doses three times daily. It is well-known that dysentery thrives mostly in malarious regions, which probably accounts for the efficacy of the cinchona. Vaseline smeared on the anus relieves to a great extent the burning and smarting of that part, and gives great relief to a distressing symptom. Rest in bed is imperative, and sponging with tepid water from time to time useful.

The last variety is best treated by sulphate of copper and opium internally, and by injections of nitrate of silver, ten to twenty grains to the ounce of water; injections thrown high up by means of a soft-rubber catheter introduced five or six inches into the rectum, the patient lying on the right side with the hips raised on a pillow. I have seen this check hæmorrhages when other means had failed. Eight ounces or more should be used at a time, the anus first thoroughly greased with vaseline. I have seen cases in which fluid extract of ergot, in half-drachm doses, given every hour, appeared to act favorably in arresting hæmorrhage from the bowel. As great weakness of the heart often occurs in this form, digitalis should be given early and continuously, with or without quinine. Bismuth and the vegetable astringents are useless, or next to it. Copper sulphate, in doses of one-sixteenth to one-twelfth grain, has, in my hands, given most satisfaction; but sometimes this remedy, even in small doses, produces vomiting, and lead will be better borne. Dysentery as an epidemic has this year been followed by cholera, and I am told it is usually so.

Nervous diseases are not so common as in countries like the United States, England, or France, where the people live under higher pressure; but they exist, especially in the form of melancholia of a suicidal tendency. Indeed, suicide seems to become epidemic in some regions. I remember one summer, in Wei Hsien, we had two or three attempted suicides daily, all from one circle of villages, and, besides those who sought us, many perished who would not seek foreign assistance. Opium, hanging, arsenic, and phosphorous matches were the favorite methods employed. " Rough on Rats " has not so far been introduced. As to demoniacal possession, I am no believer in it.

About five years ago I attended a conference in Chefoo, at the house of a missionary resident, and the above topic came in for the major part of the discussion. Being but just arrived in the country, I maintained a discreet silence, but great was my surprise to hear men of good standing arguing for the existence of demoniacal possession, and claiming that it occurred here in the East, because Satan, being so vigorously attacked in Western countries, had given up this form of persecution there, and was bestowing all his attention and energy in this portion of the globe. If I remember rightly, I was the only member of the medical profession present, and, after numerous wonderful cases had been recited by my brethren of the cloth, I was asked my professional opinion. I had a stronger opinion than I was willing to give at that time and place; so I merely said that the cases were very interesting and apparently authentic, but that, not having witnessed their peculiar symptoms, I could not pass a final opinion, and that some of them might have been mania, hysteria, etc.

I went home from the meeting with the feeling that the Chinese were not the only people who were superstitious, and that I should like very much to see some such cases as those described. For several years this privilege was denied me, but one day a man, a stupid farmer, came to the dispensary and said his young wife was possessed by a devil, and wanted some medicine. I told him I must see the case, and appointed the next day at 2 P.M. He came promptly at the hour, with his wife, aged about twenty-eight, his mother, and a male friend of the family. This friend was a curious, villainous-looking fellow, a striking contrast to the husband. I was told that when the spirit came up she would become unconscious, would tremble, sigh, and moan, and that she would remain in this condition for hours; that anger, fear, or any unpleasant emotions would bring the devil on. I asked if they had any way to invite the gentleman now, and they said they had; upon which the mother and husband stepped into the waiting-room, and the friend of the family commenced making a purring noise in his throat; immediately the poor woman cast her eyes around imploringly and became unconscious. The muscles of the throat and neck twitched violently and her head fell on her bosom. I felt her pulse; it was 76 and regular, breathing hurried and rather shallow. Was told by the friend that her attacks frequently came on in this way. On my asking how he knew in the first place that he could bring the devil up, he stuttered and stammered and took refuge in the waiting-room, upon which her mother and husband entered again. Sticking needles into her hands and arms being without avail to bring her out of this condition, I held a bottle of ammonia under her nostrils. The effect was magical; she quickly regained consciousness and soon appeared as she had been before the attack, which was simply an incomplete hysterical convulsion. Since that day I have seen several other cases of reputed demoniacal possession, and without exception they have been easily explained as the result of pathological conditions.

I think there are a good many causes for this delusion in China which do not exist in the same proportion in some other countries.

The people are mostly ignorant and superstitious, and are naturally susceptible,—fine subjects for experiments in hypnotism and suggestion. Many of these cases of possession are, doubtless, due to suggestion. Persons of susceptible temperament, seeing or hearing of others so afflicted, are tempted to worry or annoy their friends, and are carried away and frightened by their own emotions into an hysterical state bordering on actual mania.

Then, too, syphilis is no doubt responsible for some of these manifestations. Syphilis is very common among the Chinese, and, having seen a number of cases of cerebral syphilis, I cannot but believe that in many of these cases, in which erratic movements follow the natural result of the pathological condition, they are attributed to demoniacal possession.

Mania, dementia, and hysteria are sufficient of themselves to account for the cases I have either seen or heard described, and I consider any who believe in demoniacal possession as superstitious and too credible.

Epilepsy is far from infrequent, and all cases I have seen have been benefited and some apparently cured by the bromides.

Hemiplegia and paraplegia and also local paralyses are seen as a result of apoplexy or gummata making pressure on nerve-trunks. Neuralgias are very common, due to malarial and syphilitic infection in many cases, and to faulty assimilation and anæmia in others. Anæmia is very common. There is one peculiar affection, called by some observers "loss of sensation," by others "anæsthesiæ cutis," to be met with all over the North. It frequently occurs in well-nourished persons having no apparent disease. The skin on the forearm, hand, or perhaps thighs or legs, loses sensation in part or entirely. In the milder cases there is a numbness in the affected region only, but in severer cases sensation in the skin is absolutely abolished, and pins may be made to penetrate the cutis vera without exciting any pain or the patient knowing he has been pricked. The area of the affection varies greatly. Sometimes it is only the skin of a single finger or a limb, usually over one group of muscles only, as the extensors of the forearm. Stimulating liniments relieve it; whether or not they effect a cure I am unable to say definitely. Electricity is useful and, I believe, curative, in this affection, the interrupted current giving the best results. Cardiac affections are rare.

Goitre, in the neighborhood of Ch'ing Chow Fu is remarkably common, and is seen occasionally in other districts. La grippe has visited the country the past two years as an epidemic, but seemed milder than it is reported to have been in Europe.

In a country where so many dogs are maintained we would naturally expect to find rabies very frequent, but, on the contrary, it is quite rare. I met with but one case in six years.

Otorrhœa and deafness are very common. Of the cases requiring surgical treatment, none, perhaps, are more frequent than fistula in ano. Anthrax, furuncle, and abscesses are daily treated, in dispensaries, all over the empire. Tumors (benign and malignant), adenomas, fibromas, osteomas, sarcomas, epitheliomas, and carcinomas have all been diagnosed and treated by foreign surgeons, and exist here in about the same proportion as in civilized lands. Elephantiasis is quite common. Fractures and wounds, owing to the absence of railroads and machinery, are seldom seen.

The Chinese bear surgical operations exceedingly well, and it is rare for high inflammation to follow operative interference. Urinary calculus is very frequent in and around Canton, and is met with occasionally all over the empire. Owing to the Chinese being unable to treat this affection, these stones sometimes attain enormous size before they are removed by the foreign surgeon. In February, 1889, I removed, by the lateral perineal operation, a stone larger than a turkey's egg, weighing nearly three ounces when dry, and considerable, in the shape of powder, was lost in washing out the bladder. The patient, a farmer aged twenty-five, was entirely well in three weeks.

There are no skilled obstetricians among the Chinese. Male physicians would lose their reputation if they attended a woman in confinement, and so the obstetrical work is left entirely to old women, who act as midwives, receiving the child at birth and severing the cord. The infant is then wrapped in a cloth, or roll of cotton, and remains unwashed for a week. Should a shoulder-presentation or impaction of the head occur, turning or instrumental assistance is not forthcoming, and the patient always dies, worn-out, with the infant unborn. According to etiquette, a woman must not leave her own premises within a month after confinement.

CHAPTER IX.

LEPROSY cannot be as contagious or infectious as a great many alarmists, in and outside the medical profession in the United States, would have us believe; for if so, the people of China would have disappeared from the face of the earth, from leprosy, long ago. My reason for this statement lies in the fact, that although there is leprosy existing in every province of the empire and every city of size, yet, in spite of the fact that the leper is under no quarantine regulation of any kind, leprosy has not spread to any appreciable degree in the last century. If leprosy is actively contagious, would not the leper, handling money, farm-implements, and even food-products, be a centre for the distribution of the disease? In other countries, where cleanliness is more universal, a leper would not have the same opportunity of infecting others; but in China, where the money is so filthy and so much handled, to say nothing of any other means of communication of the disease, if it were of the highly infectious type, the disease would soon be general.

One of the first references to leprosy in Chinese history occurs in " Pei Wen Yun Fu," where Yü Rang painted his body with varnish, to impersonate a leper,— removing his beard and eye-brows, with the intention of so disguising himself that he might assassinate the Duke of Ts'ao, murderer of his master, Duke Tsin.

Dr. Edkins, of Peking, has studied the old Chinese histories in regard to the existence of leprosy in early times, and I quote from a recent article of his. In the calendar of seasons ("Yueh Ling") contained in the "Li Chi" it is said, "If in the middle month of winter the proceedings of government proper to spring were observed, locusts would appear and work harm, springs would all become dry, and many people would suffer from itch and leprosy." This calendar contains no small amount of superstition on the subject of luck. It says that if the proceedings of government are not regulated by the calendar all sorts of physical evils will ensue. These evils are stated, month by month. Such was the state of Chinese opinion when it was written, but when was that? The month meant was December, for it is said that the shortest day of the year occurred in the same month. The writer regarded this class of diseases as abounding specially at that time.

"This calendar is also found in the 'Ch'un T'sieu' of Lü Pu Wei, whose work dates from the third century before Christ. But the commission of learned men who wrote for Lü Pu Wei used Chow phraseology and Chow documents, as is seen in the way they speak of the feudal barons, who must have been still in existence. We may regard this calendar as very much a Chow-dynasty production. It recognizes the emperors of antiquity. It speaks of the empire as consisting of nine provinces. Further, this ancient fragment gives the place of the meridian stars at an interval of fifteen degrees in advance of the point where they are stated to have been observed by the ancient astronomers. For instance, in the 'Shu Ching,' Hsü (a star in Aquarius) is said to have been the meridian star at evening twilight in September. In the 'Yueh Ling' it is the meridian star at evening twilight in October. But the stars move at the rate of fifty second in a year, or a degree in seventy-two years. They move therefore, fifteen degrees in ten hundred and eighty years, and this position of the star Hsü in October agrees, therefore, with the age of the commencement of the Chow dynasty, or about B.C. 1100. Consequently, this testimony in regard to leprosy may possibly go back as far as the time of Chow Kung (B.C. 1100). Yet, while the astronomy is that of this date, the book, as a whole, is more likely to belong to an age some centuries later, because the 'five emperors' are mentioned as being worshiped, and the mythology has the appearance of being that of about the ninth century before Christ. We may then, at least, say that leprosy was probably known in China in the age of the later classics, two or three centuries before Confucius, and was dreaded as a calamity sent to punish moral evil.

"In the Shih Chi history there is a case of a prince, named Siang, who received the title of Marquis Yi. He became a leper and had to go home, after resigning his command. This was about B.C. 150. He lived as a leper about twenty-three years. This took place in Shantung, in T'sao Chow Fu.

"In the old history of the P'ang dynasty it is said that a woman of T'sao Chow, in Shantung, professed to have communications with demons and with nature, and to be able to cure diseases through these communications. Many lepers came to her for cure, and were healed.

"In the time of Confucius one of his own pupils (Pê Nieu) was a leper, and died of this disease. He is mentioned in the 'Lun Yü.' This incident belongs to Shantung,—in the fifth century before Christ.

"Coming down to the fourth and fifth centuries after Christ, we find traces of leprosy in South China and in

Cambodia. In the country near Soochow a somewhat conspicuous character, named Chow Hing Sï, became a leper. In his case white swellings appeared first on his hands. The Chinese divide tumors into white and red. The red are those of the light element, *Yang*; the white are those of the dark element, *Yin*. This would naturally be white leprosy. After this, continues the account, he contracted leprosy, and his left eye was soon gone. The Emperor touched his hand and sighed, saying, in the words of Confucius, 'Such a man, and to have such a disease!' The Emperor, then, with his own hand, wrote a prescription for white tumor, and gave it to him.

"'In Cambodia' it is said that 'many lepers are found. The people do not avoid them or refuse to eat with them, or even to sleep with them. The reason of this is said to be that the ruler of the country, in one instance, was a leper, and the people ceased, on this account, to feel dislike to it.' This is taken from a book on Cambodia, written at a time when the Chinese Empire usually embraced that country.

"The Taoists professed to be able to cure leprosy by charms. In the catalogue of the Sui-dynasty library there is the name of a volume on the cure of leprosy by a charm said to have been found in the cave of Lao Chiun. This was in the sixth century.

"Leprous baldness is mentioned in the Liao history. In Eastern Thibet, adjoining the province of Kan Su, there was formerly a great love of revenging injuries. When there was a time of mourning it was not right to strike any one. People wore a coat of mail, having a border as a sign. When enemies were reconciled, the blood of fowls, dogs, and pigs was mixed with wine.

This compound was stored in a skull, for drinking at the time of taking an oath. The oath was administered with the words, 'If you should again revenge yourself on such a person, may your grain be unproductive, may your sons and daughters be bald with leprosy, your cattle die, and serpents enter your tent.'

" In the 'Shen i Chiang' (Book of Marvels), of about the fifth century, a cure for leprosy is mentioned: ' The shoots of the weeping bamboo (" ti'chu "), if eaten, will cure of ulcers and leprosy.'

" In the sixth century there is a story of a city magistrate whose court-house was burnt down with his dwelling. He took refuge in a monastery, and an ox and some wine were brought by the inhabitants of the city as presents. The magistrate ordered the ox to be tied to the pillar in front of the monastery. He then caused a daïs to be prepared, and sat in his official robes in the hall to receive guests. The ox, loosening the rope with which he was tied, came across to where the magistrate was sitting, and made a bow. The magistrate laughed loudly, and at once ordered his attendants to slaughter the animal. After a hearty meal and deep potations, he lay down under the eaves to take rest. After a time he woke up with frightful sensations of itching; scratching was useless, for he had become a leper."

In the south of China, in the neighborhood of Canton, there are reported to be leper villages where those afflicted with the disease very badly are compelled to go and remain. In the North there are no such villages. The leper is privileged to go and come as he pleases, and the disease, while looked upon by the people as contagious, in some mysterious way, yet is not so powerfully so as to demand the segregation of the leper class.

In every city of any size, and many of the villages, lepers are to be seen moving about among the healthy, buying, selling, and in no way deprived of the freedom accorded the unafflicted. The disease is called the " Ta Ma Feng," which means the great benumbing disease. I have treated thirty-five cases of variable severity, from the mildest, in which the eyebrows were just falling out and sensation deficient in the forearm of one hand, to those in which ridges of copper-colored hypertrophic elevations of skin covered the face, and loss of joints, with contractions of the tendons, had occurred. In nearly every case the parents or uncles, aunts or grand-parents had, some one or more, died of the disease. The youngest patient was eighteen, the oldest forty-five, and all were men. The fact of the disease, as seen by me, having been exclusively among the male sex is explained somewhat by the knowledge that, owing to the seclusion of women in China, the great majority of my patients have been men. But, in a dispensary practice of over thirty-five thousand patients during six years, at least 10 per cent. were women; and, so far, I have not seen a case among the female sex. Dr. Cantlie, of Hong Kong, in a report of one hundred and twenty-five cases of leprosy, had as many as thirteen female patients, or a little over 10 per cent. Other observers in China also note the preponderance of male subjects having the disease. The native physicians recognize its incurable nature, and usually decline to treat it. At the present time, when the disease is much discussed and little understood, any light which can be thrown on the subject should not be withheld. The profession in China are meeting with the disease every day, but so far little has been written by them upon the subject. What has appeared has been in the form of notes, in the reports of hospitals and dispensaries, and, so far as I know, no attention has been given to expressions of opinion as to the etiology of the disease. I believe, from what I have seen, that the disease is hereditary in most cases; that it is feebly contagious; that it is inoculable. Many of my patients with leprosy have acknowledged having had syphilis, and I believe that the previous saturation of the body with syphilis affords a favorable soil for the development of the disease.

I recently heard a lecture by Dr. Formad, of Philadelphia, before the Montgomery County Medical Society of Pennsylvania, in which he stated that a bacillus, of any kind whatsoever, required a certain soil for its development and growth, one kind requiring one soil, another a different quality of soil. Given a proper soil, and the bacillus is introduced, the specific disease would be certain to follow. Introduce it upon a barren or uncongenial soil, and the death of the bacillus would follow. This proposition seems undeniable, reasoning from analogy. If it is so, the syphilitic body seems a very favorable soil for the growth of the bacillus of leprosy. The Hawaiian Islanders were a strong, hardy race, apparently, up to the time the whalers from the Pacific infected the people with syphilis, which spread until it is reported they were about all syphilized; then leprosy took hold, and to-day the settlement of Molokai, the largest leper settlement in the world, is the result. Quite a number of the cases of leprosy I have read about as occurring in the islands of the Indian Sea, Singapore, and Hong Kong, among foreigners, have been in individuals living immoral lives, and who supposed they contracted it from intercourse with Chinese,

Malay, or Eurasian prostitutes. Such individuals were, doubtless, previously syphilitic. I do not want to be understood as saying all lepers are syphilitic. My position is that a syphilitic person is more apt to become leprous upon exposure to contagion for a length of time than an otherwise healthy individual would be. The period of incubation of the disease is placed by various authorities to be from three to twenty years. I believe in heredity, and that the disease may skip one generation and appear in the next. Two of my patients stated that their grandfathers had succumbed to the disease, but their parents had never had it; consequently, I believe that the incubation may extend through a life-time.

Some authorities say that there may be such a thing as a hereditary predisposition transmitted without the transmission of the actual disease. I prefer to believe in the actual transmission of the disease, as it is more probable, and not so far-fetched an idea. That it is feebly contagious there seems no reason to doubt. Father Damien perished after nine years of continuous contact with lepers. Doubtless, during the ulcerative stage it is more contagious than at other times, owing to the discharge of morbid material directly into the atmosphere. Washer-women of lepers would be more exposed at such times than when the disease was confined to anæsthetic affection of the skin. The question of how the disease originated in any given case is always uncertain if heredity does not account for it, and it cannot account for all the cases. One case came to my knowledge where a nephew wore his uncle's hat after the latter's death from leprosy, and within two years himself became leprous. If this case was caused by wearing the hat, the incubation was of two years' dura tion; but, as he was of the same blood, the disease was more likely to have developed independently of wearing the uncle's hat. A hat-band, however, would likely be an active agent in producing infection. It receives directly the secretions of the skin upon an absorbent surface, and, upon drying, retains them; remoistened with perspiration and the friction, more or less constant, in wearing the hat, the secretion is rubbed into the skin, and actual inoculation is accomplished. As to varieties, I believe in only one variety. Other diseases are often mistaken for it, causing confusion in diagnosis; but leprosy is similar to syphilis,—there is only one variety.

True it is, however, like syphilis it may present very different manifestations in the course of years in the same subject, and in different subjects may appear very dissimilar. In some cases it runs its course in two years, but, in many, a fatal termination does not take place until more than a decade after the initial symptoms. All observers agree that, under good hygienic surroundings and proper treatment, the course of the disease may be greatly retarded and even improvement take place. The treatment embraces both constitutional and local remedies.

The constitutional remedies which have undoubted value are the tonics, vegetable and mineral. Combinations of iron, quinine, and strychnia, syrup of the hypophosphites, cod-liver oil, and the mineral acids all have their advocates. My own experience leads me to prefer the syrup of the iodide of iron in most cases as a constitutional alterative tonic. Dr. Cantlie praises very highly the ointment of Unna. He says he has seen decided improvement take place in one week, and after a short course the patient loses symptoms of leprosy. This ointment is:—

R Chrysarobin, ... 5 per cent.
Salicylic acid,. . . . 2 "
Ichthyol, ... 5 "

Where the ointment is used on the face, pyrogallol is used instead of chrysarobin, and the ointment is weakened by adding lard, 88 per cent. When pyrogallol is used, dilute hydrochloric acid should be given in ten-drop doses three times daily, to counteract the deleterious effect of the pyrogallol upon the blood. This treatment is asserted to prove rapidly ameliorative, but no claim that it is curative has been made.

In my own cases I have used an ointment of carbonate of zinc for the ulcerative process, with good results. In the worst cases I have used hydrarg. ammoniat., zinc oxid., and plumbi acet., made up into an ointment with cosmoline. I do not believe it necessary to place lepers in a special hospital when they can be well taken care of at home, and isolated to the extent of having a separate room, special dishes, and special wash-house. This is, however, as a rule, not convenient, and the leper is better off in a well-regulated hospital than in his home. I was five days the guest of a leper, on whose brother I operated for urinary calculus, and although he ate in another room he was frequently in my room, and even sat beside me on the same bench. If I believed the disease as virulently contagious as many (who have never seen a case), I should have been most unhappy at that time. I will give the notes on two typical cases that have come under my observation, and with them dismiss the subject:—

CASE I. Wang Tei Shĕng, aged 37, resides in Ch'i Hsia; farmer; father died of leprosy at the age or 45; mother died of fever last year; father's uncle died of leprosy many years ago; has two brothers younger than himself, both strong and well; has had no sisters; has heard that there is a leper in a village three miles away, but does not know him; no other leper in his own village; contracted syphilis at 21 years of age, married at 23, and has never had a living child; his wife, who is healthy, has had five miscarriages. Patient is 5 feet 8 inches tall and weighs 148 pounds; first noticed three years ago a numbness of the thumb of the left hand which in course of a few months extended to the elbow; six months later right hand became affected and eyebrows fell out; was treated by native physicians, but did not improve; a year ago right foot became anæsthetic, and a few months ago an ulcer appeared under ball of right great toe, which still exists. On examination, found that the sensation of left forearm is totally abolished and skin is dry and scaly. Right forearm, on palmar surface, still retains sensation, though diminished; dorsal surface abolished. Sensation diminished in both legs, worse on right side. A round, perforating ulcer, size of a half-dollar, exists under ball of great toe of right foot, which exposes the joint and shows the bone denuded of periosteum; left foot intact. A small ulcer, caused, he says, by carrying burdens slung on a pole, exists over the left clavicle, but, as it is not sensitive, must be regarded as suspicious; no infiltration as in gummata, only a whitish, indolent-looking ulcer. Eyebrows have disappeared; copper-colored ridges from arch of orbits to the hair; malar prominences insensible, white, and deadish-looking; eyes move sluggishly, and have an expression of apathy, betokening a torpor of the thinking faculty; answers questions slowly, but lucidly; has never had headache nor pain; knows he has the " ta ma fĕng," and comes to get relief "so he can feel things;" does not expect a cure.

CASE II. Li Wen Ta, coolie, aged 26 ; resides in Chi Yang; father's brother died of the "ta ma fêng;" father and mother both living and healthy; one brother died of leprosy two years ago, and patient fears he is going to die of the same disease; his brother was affected five years previous to his death, which was hastened by a beating received in a brawl; soon after his brother's death he noticed a numbness of right foot, which in a year's time became absolutely senseless; left foot is beginning the same way, though still retains sensibility; eyebrows have dropped out half-way across on each side, commencing from the nasal bone, giving him a curious expression ; says he has never had syphilis, but acknowledges to have had promiscuous intercourse; is unmarried ; no other marks on the face, but complains of a coldness between the shoulder-blades; tongue fairly clean and appetite good; bowels sluggish and skin dry. Case II is not as far developed as Case I, but is tending in the same direction.

The venereal diseases exist in China, as elsewhere in the world, as three principal affections,—gonorrhœa, chancroid, and syphilis. Gonorrhœa is the same disgusting disease everywhere, but, owing to the carelessness of the Chinese as to cleanliness, is particularly obnoxious amongst them. Many times I have seen cases where the patient allowed the discharge to drop into his loose, baggy trousers until they were saturated, taking no precaution whatever to keep his clothes clean, and only changing them when they became too offensive to himself to longer endure it. Owing to the diet being largely vegetable, however, the disease seems, in a majority of

cases, to run its acute course more rapidly, and to soon
subside into a gleet, and often disappears, after a few
days of suppuration, without any treatment. Many of
the better classes even believe it may be a result of
cold, and the wind is blamed for many a case of clap,
which, of course, it had nothing to do with. Gonor-
rhœal ophthalmia is a frequent accident, but orchitis and
epididymitis are rarely seen, considering the frequency
of the disease. When it exists among the upper classes,
it is harder to cure, as they will not obey orders about
diet, and indulge too largely in fatty foods and stimu-
lants. Chancroids are more rare and chancres more
common than in the United States. I remember, when
attending the venereal clinics of the hospitals in America,
that chancroid was much more common than the syphilitic initial lesion. In China the reverse is the case; at
least, in my experience. I have seen ten chancres where
I saw one chancroid. Syphilis is very little understood
by the native physicians. Some of them recognize pus-
tulous syphilis as due to impure intercourse, but the more
obscure manifestations of it are never attributed to the
proper cause. As it is greatly neglected, many cases of
brain syphilis come under observation, as well as bone
troubles and all the phenomena of the tertiary period.
It yields very rapidly to treatment, even in the worst
cases,—due, in my belief, to the vegetable diet of the mass
of the people. People without noses are more common
in China than in the United States. Nothing is done by
government to stamp out the disease, and brothels are
not under police or sanitary regulations, as in Japan.
The Chinese use mercury in the treatment of syphilis, in
the form of an impure calomel, given in large doses.
This produces violent purging, which is supposed to clear

out the disease. They bear iodides badly. Small doses have, in my hands, produced iodism several times, and other observers have noticed the same fact. I always go carefully in administration of the iodides, and usually commence with three grains three times daily, and increase it as I find the patient will bear it. Ulcerations of syphilitic origin exist sometimes to frightful extent, but they heal up beautifully and rapidly under appropriate treatment.

The Chinese have been accused of being great practicers of sodomy, having institutions resembling brothels where it is carried on. I am glad to say I believe these rumors are mostly false. I learned on authority of my teacher, a Mr. Yang, that there was one large place in Tientsin where boys of from ten to sixteen years of age were used for immoral and disgusting purposes, and occasional cases that have come to the dispensary prove it is occasionally carried on. But it is not a national vice, as it is in Korea, and the mention of it to an ordinary Chinaman fills him with disgust and horror. I merely mention this subject to refute the stigma some have placed upon the Chinese in this respect. As a whole, I doubt if the Chinese are in any respect more immoral than Americans or English, and, considering their light, they can well compare with many who boast of the social purity of their country. Adultery may even be punished with the death of the guilty parties, which in civilized countries is not possible. I saw a woman and her paramour led to execution down the principal street of Chinanfu, for adultery and the suspicion of having killed the woman's husband, and all around me the people kept saying, "A righteous verdict," "They deserve to die," and other like comments expressive of their disgust at the crime and their satisfaction with the extreme penalty about to be administered.

CHAPTER X.

No work professing to give any idea of the China of to-day can with fairness leave out the missionaries. It is to their labors the world at large is indebted for a knowledge of its language, customs, and thought. It is they who have penetrated to the interior, prepared maps, translated dialects, and opened the way for the merchant and the civilizing power of contact with Western nations. It behooves every person desiring to be considered well read to have some knowledge of who the missionaries are and what they are doing. They are the representatives of the churches of all civilized and Christian nations sent to China to evangelize the country, and are nearly always well educated, refined, and courageous men and women. England, France, Germany, Italy, Denmark, Sweden, and the United States all annually send many men and women to this field. Roman Catholics, Episcopalians, Presbyterians, Methodists, Baptists, Congregationalists, Lutherans, Christian Brethren, and Temperance workers are to be found in all the provinces open to travel. Several of the most interior provinces have so far successfully resisted the settlement of missionaries within their borders, but gradually new stations are being located farther and farther from the coast, and it will not be long before active missionary work is being carried on in every province of the empire. I have heard some people say they doubted if Christianity was suitable as a religion for the Chinese, but, as they were not Christians

(169)

themselves, they were in a poor position to judge. No Christian ever doubts that Christianity is suitable for mankind, irrespective of race. But what are the results of it among the Chinese? The same as among any other nation. The first generation of Christians are weak; the second generation are stronger and better; and the third are an improvement on the second. The Romish Church has realized this fact, and established the principle of not ordaining any of the first or second generation to the priesthood.

It is an exceptional thing to see strong, reliable, Christian character developed in a man converted from heathenism late in life, though it sometimes is undoubtedly the case. Usually more or less of the superstitions of heathenism are blended with his belief in the new religiou of Yě Su. Many seek the missionaries and profess conversion in the hope of obtaining employment. Sooner or later they are found out and expelled from the churches, but their evil example is sufficient to cause much talk and throw discredit upon the cause. This is a result of admitting a man to church membership before he really understands all that is expected of him or what Christianity requires. Formerly nearly all the denominations only required a profession of faith to admission to church membership. Now, after having been frequently victimized, they require a knowledge of the person's character and motives, and the candidate is kept on probation for periods varying from six months to several years. The mistakes of the earlier missionaries are lessons to the later ones, and the work is more successful now than formerly, because the people are better understood and missionary methods better adapted to them.

The introduction of medical men, with dispensaries and hospitals, into missionary work is a comparatively recent thing; but to-day it is proved not only in China, but throughout the world, to be an effectual way of reaching many not otherwise susceptible. Christ's method of combining the healing of the body with the preaching of the Word experience proves cannot be improved upon. There are some who scoff at the missionaries and ridicule them on all occasions. I have taken pains to investigate many of the charges they made, and invariably found them false. Then I turned my investigations upon the accusers themselves, and found in every instance that the lives of the missionary scoffers were such as no Christian man could lead. Men in the ports, who keep mistresses, break the Sabbath, use profane language, and get drunk, can always tell you what wicked, lazy, expensive nuisances missionaries are. Ask them when they have been to the missions, when they visited country stations, when they personally inspected mission work, and they cannot answer. Missionaries receive from the various Boards of Foreign Missions salaries ranging from three hundred to seven hundred dollars per individual annually. Five hundred dollars is perhaps the average annual salary of a single missionary, or one thousand dollars for a man and his wife. Many, however, receive much smaller salaries, and a few somewhat larger. The majority of the missionaries are college graduates, though some, as in the China Inland Mission, are people of limited education. These, being unused to habits of study, rarely acquire the language as perfectly as the college student, and are, in consequence, always laboring under that disadvantage. All Mission Boards require examinations in the language at stated intervals, and persons unable to acquire a working knowledge of it are returned home as incapable for work.

Missionaries are not allowed to retain fees for services rendered either to the Chinese or others. All moneys received in this way are turned into the respective treasuries. Medical missionaries are no exception to this rule. Missionary work at the present day may be classed as clerical, medical, and educational. Clerical work is that performed by the ordained preacher, and consists of street-chapel preaching, itineration, and conversational. In every port city and in many of the large cities of the interior a clergyman will rent a building or shop on a thoroughfare and use it as a street-chapel, as it is called, which means that every day of the week he and his native helpers will take turns in preaching to whoever will stop and listen. Usually Bibles or portions of Scripture are given away gratis at such places. This is the method that all new-comers like best, but statistics prove it to be least productive in results. Very few missionaries who have lived many years in the country can be found to speak well of this method. They say the people are too busy to listen attentively, and the audience is constantly changing, making such confusion that, with the noise from the street added, no one has a fair chance to hear. Then, too, work in the cities does not yield the result in converts that work in the country districts does. The missionaries who have been most successful have devoted the larger part of their energies to itinerative trips to the country. In these itinerations the missionary visits the villages of the interior, remaining in one place from a few hours to several days, and then moving on to another point where some interest

A Group of Shantung School-Girls.

has been manifested. Some missionaries make long trips, being away from home and their families for three months at a time. Travel is so slow that a journey of three hundred miles, stopping at the principal villages of a circuit, would require that time to complete. Much effectual work is done by the conversational method. First making an acquaintance, then a visitor and friend of a man, and gradually, as he ceases to be afraid of you, open up to him the truth of the Gospel.

As the seclusion of women presents a strong barrier to work among them by male missionaries, the wives of ministers and physicians, with single ladies and lady physicians, are used as a means of reaching them. This field, to my mind, offers the most hopeful work of all. Christianize the mothers and sisters, and the men will not remain heathen. Frequently the strongest opposition to a man's becoming a Christian is from the women of his household. The work of the lady missionaries cannot be too highly commended. Many of them live far in the interior, away from all the luxuries and many of the necessaries of civilization, spending their days in going from village to village or town to town, teaching the women of China the " doctrine " of Christ. They are not ignorant fanatics, but highly-educated, earnest, thoughtful, Christian women. They are seldom insulted and never molested, and find an entrance by their sympathies into the homes of the peasant and sometimes the prince.

Some who will not see the use of clerical work will admit the value of medical work among the Chinese, independent of its connection with the salvation of the race. An atheist with whom I conversed during our trip across the Pacific, a fellow-passenger, said to me, "Well, I can see the good of medical work among the Chinese, or any other race who have no scientific knowledge of the treatment of disease. It is humanitarian, and as such I would subscribe to it; but not a cent for the spread of the Gospel." Medical missionaries are treated more considerately by the Chinese than the clerical, and frequently a medical man obtains valuable concessions for his mission that would not be granted to the clergymen alone. Western medicine, and especially surgery, are winning golden opinions in the Celestial Empire. Wherever a mission dispensary or hospital is established, prejudice against the foreigner gradually abates. A brilliant surgical operation is regarded by the Chinese as miraculous and is reported for miles away, increasing in the miraculous element with distance.

In starting medical work in a new field, usually a small shop is rented and opened as a free dispensary. After opposition—which is sure to arise—has subsided, a hospital is started, and soon friends of the doctor abound; if not of his colleagues, the clergymen.

Much care has to be exercised in the selection of cases for operation at first, as an unsuccessful or fatal operation in a new field would have a very detrimental effect on not only the medical work, but all branches of mission work at that point. Poisons have to be given dose at a time, otherwise ten days' medicine might be taken at one dose and a fatal result follow. Medical missionaries itinerate as well as their clerical colleagues, sometimes in company with them. A sure way to build up a fine practice and reputation in any given city is to itinerate through all the surrounding villages, visiting and prescribing for the sick, drawing teeth, and performing minor operations, at the same time telling where you may be found in the city. I say fine practice, not lucrative practice, for a medical missionary does not retain and seldom charges fees. He devotes his profession to the relief of pain, the healing of disease, the advancement of his noble profession, and, last and greatest of all, as a means of spreading the truth of God's Word. Many are incredulous of the fact that there are men whose aim is above making money or reputation in the profession of medicine. If such would take the pains to acquaint themselves with the facts, they would be convinced that such is the case.

There are surgeons in China, such as Dr. J. G. Kerr in Canton (who has operated on more cases of stone in the bladder than any living man), Dr. Boone in Shanghai, Dr. Atterbury in Peking, Dr. Peck in Pang Chuang, and many others too numerous to mention, who have deliberately relinquished, for the small salary of a medical missionary and a share in the work of winning China to Christendom, the emolument practice at home was sure to give them. Cases of rare interest are constantly presenting themselves at the mission hospitals, and the medical missionary who is in love with his profession has abundant opportunity to study disease in all its varied forms. Neglected cases, such as we never see in civilized lands, are met with every day. The missionaries of all branches of work are an immense power for civilization in the amount of information they impart. The Chinese are always asking questions, and the information about civilized lands and methods thus imparted and spread by means of conversation cannot be estimated. It is second only to what a daily paper would be if much read.

The educational work consists in schools for both

sexes established in various places, and in the inquirers' classes instituted from time to time at the residences of the missionaries. The Romanists, too, have orphan asylums, and, so far as I know, are the only denomination who have thus far taken up that branch of the work. Nearly all of the schools teach all studies, such as geography, history, arithmetic, algebra, geometry, and reading and writing, in the Chinese language, by means of translated books. The reading is chiefly the native classics, the time-honored works of Confucius, Mencius, and their disciples. Some of the schools in the port cities teach English, and the recently-opened Methodist University in Peking teaches medicine and theology in English.

The Chinese government has established several schools for the acquirement of Western learning, the principal ones being the Tung Wen College, of Peking, of which Rev. Dr. Martin, a Presbyterian minister, is president, and the Tientsin College of Sciences, of which Rev. Mr. Tenney is president. The Chinese authorities recognize the fact that the missionaries, acquainted with the language and people, are the best adapted to superintend these institutions. In the mission schools preference is given to children of Christian parents among applicants, though children of heathen parents are also accepted. The Tung Chow College, for a long time under the superintendence of Rev. Dr. Mateer, and now under Rev. W. M. Hayes, has over one hundred students. The course is a full college course, and embraces the higher mathematics and chemistry, all taught in Chinese from translated books. Rev. Dr. Porter has translated a book on physiology; Dr. Dudgeon, an English medical missionary, has translated

Gray's "Anatomy;" Dr. Kerr has translated Bartholow's "Practice of Medicine," a work on surgery, another on chemistry, and still another on venereal diseases. Dr. Hunter has translated a materia medica and pharmacopœia.

Almost without exception the works translated into Chinese have been the work of missionaries. Can any one ask if the missionaries have done any good? The Bible has been translated into the Wĕn Li, or highest style classical language; the Mandarin, or official language; the Ning Po, Foo Chow, and many other local dialects. Tracts, Sunday-school books, and papers are being constantly printed from the mission presses in Shanghai and Peking. Scientific literature is being disseminated with religions by the missionaries, and every effort is made to disclose to this nation the result of centuries of progress by other lands. Missionary labors will be greatly lightened when the introduction of railroads makes travel more endurable than at present. More effort is being made each year to educate young men in the theological schools of the various missions to take the place of the foreign missionary. They can do equally good work, create less disturbance owing to lack of race prejudice, and live at much less expense.

In time China must be evangelized by native clergy, and the work of the foreign missionary will become more and more of an educational work as years pass, leaving the itinerating and man-to-man work to the trained native, who is better fitted to carry it on than a man of a different race. Race prejudice is the hardest of all prejudices to overcome, and the European or Anglo-Saxon will always be at a disadvantage working among the Orientals. Change of dress, perfection in the language,

—above all, a sympathetic fellow-feeling,—may do much to remove the barrier, but never can an Anglo-Saxon become as near to the Chinese as one of their own race.

It only remains to do all that can be done in that direction, regarding them and treating them as men and brothers, and placing an educated body of trained native clergy in the field to carry on work effectually that can but partially be done by foreigners. The church in the future in China will not be of Anglo-Saxon mold; it will be an essentially Chinese mold, and so we should desire it. "Give them Christ's Gospel and leave the formation of the details of church government to work out in time into that form which best suits the Oriental mind," is the opinion of all the ablest, broadest, and most evangelical ministers and missionaries cognizant of the field.

CHAPTER XI.

In order to make money in China several things have to be taken into consideration:—

1. The circumstances of the population. It is not a rich country. There are, undoubtedly, a number of very wealthy families in the empire, but, as compared with the total population, not nearly so numerous as in America or England. The great majority of its inhabitants will not average fifteen cents a day income. The government is also poor, and has difficulty to meet actual expenses and pay the interest on its small bonded debt. The government, however, could greatly increase its income by the development of mining and manufacturing interests, and foreign capitalists will furnish money whenever called upon to build railroads or open mines, knowing that the returns will enable the government to meet all obligations incurred. At present agriculture and business pursuits are the principal occupations of the middle and laboring classes. Introduce mining and manufacturing, and the whole country will assume an improved aspect.

2. Foreigners are not allowed to do business in the interior, or indeed to reside at all in some of the provinces. This cannot at present be overcome; but later on, when the people have become more educated in regard to Western nations, we may expect this prohibition to be removed. The port cities are now open to foreigners to reside in and engage in business, and some of them are making princely fortunes in importing goods desirable to the Chinese, and exporting tea, straw-braid, silk, etc.

(179)

In the present undeveloped condition of the country only such articles will be salable as meet a popular demand and are of low price, the seller depending on enormous sales at small profits rather than large profits on few sales. True, there are many articles and goods used in the United States that would command a sale if introduced into China; but they have not so far been introduced, and their introduction means time, advertisement, and pushing. It is easier usually to supply an already-existing demand than to create a new one. There is no prohibition to any class desiring to do business or obtain employment in the port cities; citizens or subjects of any nationality may come at their pleasure.

Whether in obtaining contracts from the government, or large Chinese firms, or in private business operations, the maxim that honesty is the best policy should ever be observed. The Chinese have, as a rule, found English and American business men to be entirely honorable and trustworthy, and I rejoice in the reputation the Anglo-Saxon has made in the East in this regard; but there have been instances in which the Chinese have been duped on a large scale by adventurers from England and the United States, and they are becoming suspicious of their reputation for honesty. I knew a man who was paid five hundred dollars a month and expenses by a Chinese firm to go to the United States and buy a mining plant, the firm believing that he would obtain it for them at the lowest possible price. He bought an outfit for $20,000, had the bills made out as $38,000, and pocketed the difference, besides a year's salary and a handsome gift for his honesty. After his departure the firm found out how he had swindled them, and are now very incredulous of the honesty of Americans.

3. The language is so difficult that few in business in China ever take the trouble to learn the language, but depend, instead, on interpreters and compradors, as they are called. These rascals are thieves of the highest order. They swindle their employer so openly that if he knew but very little of the language he would easily see how he is being robbed. Sometimes, indeed, the employer knows he is being badly squeezed, but sees no way out of it. If he would trouble himself to study a few hours a day, he would be able to do much himself that he otherwise has to trust to his comprador; but even if he is perfect master of the language, he will often be swindled by his overconfidence in or misunderstanding of the man he is dealing with. Some business men say they are less swindled by their comprador, who is a rogue, than they would be if they were obliged to deal with all the rogues themselves. But if a man understands the language thoroughly, his comprador is obliged to be more circumspect, and cannot swindle as openly nor as badly as where his employer is totally ignorant of the language. In small business undertakings a man need not have a comprador; one or more clerks speaking a little English will answer the purpose, and can be hired cheaply. But all such will have to be closely watched. Many stories have I heard of how these clerks and English-speaking servants were so good, faithful, and honest, that, finally, after a year or more, their employer trusts them with large sums at a time, and, when the sum is large enough, the honest, faithful, and good boy departs and is never heard of again.

As I have stated in another chapter, railroads are the most pressing needs of the empire. It seems really absurd, when you look at it, that in an empire of such

size and importance as China there should only be one
small railroad of a few miles in extent existing at the
present day.   Why does not China have railroads ?   In
answer to this question you will be told that the people
are too superstitious ; that they are afraid the passage
of engines would interfere with the " feng shui ; " would
disturb the spirits of their ancestors, by passing near or
over their graves, etc.   These reasons were valid enough
twenty or more years ago, but are only put forward now
by those in power to hide the real cause of opposition to
the construction of the iron roads.   The Chinese, while
acknowledging the vast utility of railroads as a commercial agency, and their value in the transportation of
troops in time of war, are preventing their construction,
on one pretense or another, simply from jealousy of this
official to that official being given power to construct,
and, consequently, power to squeeze, and so make an
immense fortune for himself.   Two years ago, when Li
Hung Chang, the wise and patriotic Viceroy of Chih Li,
obtained the consent of the Emperor to the construction
of a road from Hankow to Peking, the papers and foreign residents of China were all rejoiced that this sluggish land had awakened to a necessity for her preservation as an empire, and for the advancement of her
business interests.   But, no.   Chang Chih Tung, the
Viceroy of the Canton Provinces, could not afford to let
the glory of introducing railroads on such a large scale
rest with his rival, Li Hung Chang; so he petitioned the
throne that, whereas, if foreign capital and foreign skill
were employed in the construction of the road, all
moneys paid therefor would be carried from the country,
and the country be much poorer ; and, whereas, China
could produce all the necessary materials for the construc-

tion of such a road; therefore, let the road be built, even as his Majesty, the Son of Heaven, had wisely decreed; but let it be also decreed that the capital furnished be by Chinese subjects, the iron used of Chinese manufacture, and the coal necessary from Chinese mines, etc. This petition, being backed by all of the friends of Viceroy Chang and all the enemies of Viceroy Li, was too powerful to be disregarded; so his Majesty was obliged to issue a decree which virtually stops the railroads for some time at least, because there is no plant in China producing iron or steel rails, the mines are not properly worked, and the coal is so far from the iron that the carriage of the coal on mule-back or by wheelbarrows makes the expense of development too great to be thought of.

Viceroy Li retaliated in the only way in his power, viz.: He apparently acquiesced in Viceroy Chang's ultrapatriotic scheme, and nominated Viceroy Chang to be given charge of the development of the railroad interests in accordance with the native-production plan, and suggested his transfer to the viceroyalty of the two Hu provinces, as the railroad must commence from there. This has been done, and now Viceroy Chang has been changed to Hankow, and has charge of the development of the Hankow-Peking railroad scheme, which, if he adheres to his original idea, will ultimately work his ruin.

This restriction of control to a native superintendent is fatal to the development of railroads, owing to the lack of confidence the people have in their rulers. There is abundance of capital in China. There are many rich merchants and rich officials who could and would furnish the capital to build railroads if they had any security that the money would be expended carefully for plant and construction; but they know from experience that to entrust it to a Chinaman is to line his pockets with it, beyond which there is little result. If it were not that Russia is pushing her railroad across Siberia night and day, this deadlock in China might exist indefinitely, and railroads be years in spanning the empire; but in the uneasiness with which the question is constantly asked, " How are the Russians progressing with the Siberian railroad?" you have an index to the Chinese mind on the subject, and can see that the fruit of it will be that the people, frightened into a reality of their danger of invasion, will break down all reserve and hastily set about constructing the necessary roads for strategic purposes. How successful they will be will depend to considerable extent on the tardiness of their awakening. There have for years been representatives of English and German syndicates in China, trying to obtain contracts or concessions from the Chinese government for the construction of railroads, but so far they have signally failed. This cannot remain so much longer. Sooner or later the ice will be broken, and with a country as large as the United States, and much more thickly populated, the extent of the railroads to be built will be something hard to realize.

No wonder that some European firms have kept well-paid representatives in China for years, so as not to lose any opportunity of obtaining precedence in this work. I have met representatives of several firms, English and German, who were trying to secure contracts from China, but, curiously enough, none of them could speak a word of Chinese. They were obliged to depend on interpreters, and were often misinformed and misled

General Chang Kao Yuan, Military Commander of East Shantung.

by the ignorance, carelessness, or untrustworthiness of their interpreters. American firms bidding for Chinese contracts should have American representatives well-versed in the Chinese language if they desire to obtain the plum.

At present the most pressing need exists for a railroad between Shanghai and Peking, tapping the large cities of Chin Kiang, Chining Chow, Chinanfu, and Tientsin, besides many cities of minor importance. This road would enable merchandise to move northward and southward in winter-time; whereas at present, from the time of ice-forming, sometimes as early as November, until breaking-up in February, the Pei Ho is blocked and steamers no longer visit Tientsin. This road would be seven hundred and fifty miles in extent, and, this line once built, an equal necessity would be felt for a road from Chining Chow eastward to Chefoo, tapping the Shantung promontory. This road would pass through the prosperous cities of Huang Hsien, Lai Chow, Wei Hsien, Ch'ing Chow, Chang Loa, Chow Tsun, Chinanfu, and Tai An, and would be three hundred and sixty miles long.

The Emperor has already sanctioned the road from Hankow to Peking, over six hundred miles in extent, but, as already stated, owing to the interference of Viceroy Chang, is held in abeyance. As soon as that gentleman realizes that he cannot complete his task with native resources, he will retire and another more progressive man will give the contract to a foreign syndicate and the work will go on. The coast cities of Canton, Amoy, Foochow, Ning Po, and Shanghai will require binding together by the iron rails and necessitate the building of nine hundred miles of road. All these routes are near the coast. The great interior cities have not even been mentioned. Railroad-builders, keep your eyes open.

Besides railroad-building there are other opportunities for foreigners in the Celestial Kingdom. Mines exist in abundance which are now only worked by manual labor. Selling mining machinery and teaching the Chinese to use it is an opening that is already beginning to be appreciated. Agricultural machinery and implements will never be much required, for the majority of their farms are so small and labor so cheap that even an American plow would be too dear for the poor farmer to think of purchasing. Matches are greatly appreciated, but are supplied so cheaply from Vienna that it is doubtful if foreigners could profitably manufacture them in China. But a firm has recently started to manufacture them in Tientsin, which, if successful, will doubtless be followed by other factories in different parts of the empire. Dentists are beginning to be appreciated by the Chinese, and a first-class dentist locating in any of the open port cities is sure of abundant patronage. At present a few dentists in Shanghai and Hong Kong have the monopoly of all China, and they charge exorbitant prices. Good salaries to clerks are paid in all the business-houses at the ports, and promotion is sure to follow with years of service. Engineers on steamers are always in demand and are paid good wages. Scotch engineers predominate along the coast of China, but America has not a few also. Navigators also obtain good wages and usually rapid promotion.

Western medicines have won their way to favor, and proprietary medicines, if advertised properly, are sure of an enormous sale. The Chinese are pre-eminently a medicine-taking people. I scarcely ever met a man who had not some disease, real or imaginary, for which he was taking medicine. Fellows' Syrup of Hypophosphites has been much advertised, and is rapidly gaining favor with the upper classes. Condensed milk is a very popular remedy with them, and its already large sales could be greatly increased by advertising. Its use is more as a remedy than an article of diet, though many of the wealthy officials are partly substituting it for tea. American crackers in tins, if advertised, could secure an enormous sale. At present they are only used in and near the port cities, but with railroads, or even without railroads, if introduced and pushed in the interior, they would pay well.

Preserved fruits and jams have never been advertised or pushed among the Chinese, but would doubtless pay. Cheap cutlery is in demand, also plated spoons. Forks and other of our table utensils are not used, and would be a drug on the market. Wagons of foreign manufacture would be useless, in the present condition of Chinese roads; so there is no demand for them. Harness and leather goods come in the same category. Cheap mirrors are eagerly bought, as well as cheap rubber combs. A Chinaman, like any other man, longs to own a watch, and cheap watches of silver or nickel find a ready sale wherever introduced. Clocks, too, are appreciated, and every householder longs to own one. The people are commencing to speak of the time of day, in many places, by the clock, instead of by the sun or change of police-watch, as formerly. Guns and revolvers would be eagerly bought, but, as they are contraband goods, and prohibited from sale, only smuggled goods are sold at present. Lumber has for many years come from Korea alone, but recently San Francisco and Oregon have exported some lumber to China, and the openings in this business are probably numerous. Chinese nails are all wrought iron, and hard nails command a ready sale. Screws are a novelty to them, and sell like hot cakes. In fact, all hardware goods are appreciated, and sell well. Cheap lamps are in demand, as coal-oil is fast supplanting the native bean-oil, and when railroads make its transportation less risky than at present the use of coal-oil will be universal.

Life-insurance and fire-insurance are unknown, and companies starting these branches of business in the ports, with ramifications in the interior, would do a good business. The manufacture and sale of glass in panes would pay, as the demand is constantly increasing. Windows for centuries have consisted of paper alone; but recently glass has been introduced, and is becoming more and more popular. Cotton-prints and plain-blue cotton-cloth are used in incredible quantities, and at present are largely imported from the United States. If manufactured in China, using native, cheap labor, the cost could be so reduced as to undersell all present competitors and obtain control of the market, though no one house could supply the demand. One trouble at present is, that foreigners are not allowed to have business-houses in the interior. They are restricted to the port cities, and know little of the opportunities that exist in the interior in the way of business. But with a manufactory and warehouses in Shanghai or some port city, and native branch-houses established in every large city, almost any business that supplies an existing want such as those mentioned above, would have a great measure of success. It is not necessary that there should be a house run by a foreigner in the large cities other than the ports, for the native houses do very well if a little foreign energy is back of them; but a foreigner speaking Chinese fluently would have to visit the large cities and establish branch-houses amongst the most responsible of already existing native firms. There are some firms that have existed over a hundred years, and such firms can always be found if inquiry is made.

There are several firms in the city of Chinanfu, with which I am acquainted, that have been doing business at the same stand for over a hundred years. The majority of business is conducted upon the Hebrew plan, of asking two or three times what they expect to obtain; but there are firms which have advertised on their signs "No two prices." At such places it is useless to ask reduction. Foreign medical men will not for many years be able to make a living from the receipts of their practice in a purely native community. Fees are too low among the native physicians for a skilled and educated man from Western countries to compete with. Five, ten, or fifteen cents is the average price per visit obtainable in the North. The physician rides around the street upon a wheelbarrow because he cannot afford a sedan-chair.

The exclusion of Chinese from America has had very little effect so far upon the treatment of Americans in China. This is probably due to the ignorance of the Chinese in regard to foreign affairs. Outside of the province of Kuang Tung, from which all the Chinese who have come to this country have emigrated, very little is known of the exclusion bill. Millions of people in China never heard even of America, far less of Americans excluding Chinese from their country. Of course, most of the mandarins know it, and regard it as an insult to their race, and in time, if not less discriminative, this bill will injure American traffic with China. If the United States would prohibit the landing of paupers from all countries, making no distinction of color or race, the feeling that they are discriminated against would subside, and it would be recognized that the legislative enactment was simply as a measure of national defense.

CHAPTER XII.

To form any idea of the present political condition of China, it is necessary to outline her form of government. China is, apparently, an absolute monarchy, with the Emperor as absolute authority in all matters. His will decides all questions of policy. He appoints all the governors of provinces and high officers at his imperial pleasure. This is the apparent condition of things, but is it really so? No; not by any means. The Emperor is a young man, who has but recently assumed the power of government, and of whose ability to govern the world at large so far knows nothing; though, if we may judge by the wisdom his royal mother has displayed during his minority, we may expect in the future a ruler of no mean ability. But at present, hedged about with the superstitions and customs of by-gone times, confined by usage to the limits of the imperial residence in Peking, except when making a pilgrimage to the tombs of his ancestors without the city, he has no opportunity to become acquainted with the state of his own country from personal observation, to say nothing of the condition of the outside world or the powers immediately adjacent; so that the real rulers of China are the members of what is known as the Six Boards and the Tsung Li Yamen, the members of these boards being wily old mandarins who have successively and successfully passed through all the under offices, and now, by age and iniquitous experience, are entitled to guide the craft of state and circumvent each other for the few remaining years of their existence. These six boards are: The Board of War, Board of Punishments, Board of Office, Board of Ceremonies, Board of Revenue, and Board of Works. Besides these there exists a board, called the Board of Censors, whose duty it is to criticise the action of all officials of high rank, both in the capital and throughout the provinces, and they are even supposed to criticise the Emperor himself. This board, which should be the highest in rank, is inferior to any of the six boards, and its authority of very little real importance. Its principal use seems to be a convenient method of first arraigning and then disposing of officials in power, to make room for some aspiring office-seeker with more wealth. All business relating to government is done in a most formal manner, and has to go through all the red-tape, time-consuming channels before it is finally accomplished.

Indeed, in the word ceremony you have the life of officialdom. Every circumstance or contingency likely to arise is provided for and the ceremonial proper to it minutely described in the " Li Chi," or Chinese Book of Rites. When a vacancy occurs, through the death or removal of a governor of a province, the Board of Office recommends one or more names; the Emperor, assisted by his Privy Council, consisting of nine Man Ch'us and seven Chinese, who may be, and doubtless are, members of the various boards enumerated, selects the name of the party thought most fitting of those presented. Then, in a decree, the Emperor makes the appointment.

Each of the eighteen provinces of the country are ruled by a governor. Sometimes he is the highest in authority in the province,—as in the Shantung province ; in other provinces he may be second in authority, there being a viceroy in charge of two or more provinces,—as the two Hu provinces, or the two Kuang provinces.

The governor or viceroy of a province is a veritable little king, and frequently pays but slight heed to the imperial mandate, or that of the boards. He has the power of life and death, the command of troops, and about the only concern he has with the powers in Peking is to see that the assessment of taxes, apportioned as the proper levy upon his province, is annually forwarded to his imperial master. Each province collects taxes for its own expenses, pays for its own government, and maintains its own troops. The governor or viceroy is only in danger of losing his position when here are insurrections within his province or he is unable to forward the tribute—rice and silver—to Peking. So long as he can squeeze the mandarins beneath him, and they the people, within the limit of endurance, he may exercise his vice-regal authority. He may be a man of much learning in the Chinese classics, or he may be a military graduate who scarcely recognizes a character.

There was a great deal of dissatisfaction among the literary classes in Shantung, a few years back, when Chang Yao was appointed governor. They scouted the idea that a man who, as they said, did not even recognize the character *ding*, made like a letter **T** (and considered the simplest character in the Chinese language), should be appointed Governor of Shantung, the province which gave to the world the sages Confucius and Mencius. This was an exaggerated statement, as Gen. Chang Yao had won distinction in the war against the T'ai P'ings; and, although nothing of a scholar, was appointed through his friendship with Li Hung Chang.

13

A curious feature of Chinese government is, that no mandarin is allowed to hold office in his native province. Thus, a man born in Chih Li may hold office in any of the other seventeen provinces, but not in his own, and the policy of government is to remove him as far from his home as possible; so we find the magistrates in the province of Shantung to be largely from An Hui, Kuang Tung, Kuang Hsi, and Kuei Chow, in preference to the provinces of Shan Hsi, Chih Li, and Hŏ Nan, which are nearer.

The system of squeezing has a most demoralizing effect upon the people generally. Commencing with the governor, who has to pay to the authorities in Peking a handsome sum for his appointment, down to the smallest "ti fang," or village policeman, the system is universal.

A magistrate of a hsien, of which there are a hundred and ten in the province of Shantung, is supposed to receive about twelve hundred dollars per annum salary; but in a good-paying magistracy like that of Lan Shan Hsien, the principal hsien-city in I Chow Fu, the magistrate can annually pocket twenty thousand taels, equivalent to thirty thousand dollars. You may be sure, a man appointed to this hsien has to make heavy presents to the Fu T'ai (governor) and Fan T'ai (treasurer); besides, he must have a record as an expert collector (squeezer). Some hsiens (districts) that have been flooded by the Yellow River are so poverty-stricken that even the ordinary salary cannot be collected, and the taxes have to be remitted, or the people would all starve. To be appointed a magistrate to one of these districts is a calamity. The nominee dare not refuse the office when tendered him by the governor, but he accepts about as joyfully as the Japanese noble of olden times when he was informed that the Mikado would graciously allow him to perform the hari kiri.

We are told that education is more wide-spread in China, among the male population, than in any other country on the globe; for, being the *only* high road to honor and emolument, all those seeking official position must be highly educated. This I emphatically contradict. It may have been so centuries ago. Where, in America or England, can you find a village of a hundred families in which only one man can read and write? Yet, in China, I have been in numerous villages where there was not more than one educated (?) man.

And as to the so-called civil-service examinations, whose purity is preached up to Western nations as a model for them to follow, what is the actual state of affairs? It is a sham, arranged to satisfy the people with false hopes that are never fulfilled. How many poor young men of ability have toiled and studied, year after year, able to recite from memory the four books and five classics, who have attended all the examinations from the time they were eighteen until eighty, and have never obtained even their first degree, but who have seen the sons of officials, or wealthy business-men, without effort, obtain their degrees, their button of rank, and be commissioned to govern and squeeze their fellow-subjects, until they became rich! At every triennial examination in the "fu," or prefect, a few first degrees will be given to the young men from the country, but the majority will be apportioned to the sons of the ruling class, who are destined to take the places of their fathers as the governors of the "pei hsing," or people (literally, the hundred names). As to the second degree, or "chü ren," rarely indeed is this rank given to one outside the charmed circle, unless he be too old to enter as a competitor for the degree above, which would entitle him to " hou pu" (wait to fill a vacancy).

True it is that all who obtain the first two degrees cannot become officials, because there are not positions enough to go around; but they are contented with secretaryships, deputy work, and minor positions, and the hope always held out of future promotion. Jealousy of each other, mutual deceit, strife for higher rank and consequent opportunities for greater ability to squeeze, are characteristic of all Chinese mandarins. Pride and arrogance, constituents of every Chinaman's make-up, are developed in an extraordinary degree by the mandarins, and it is to this ingredient of their characters we are indebted for their hatred of foreigners. No sooner is he brought in contact with a Western gentleman than the mandarin realizes how little he knows, how little his boasted Confucian teachings will benefit him; his ignorance of geography, history, science, and business life all become patent to him, and he cries, in very shame, "Away with this foreign devil! Close our doors to him! Drive him from our shores, and let us ignore his existence!"

He echoes this cry to his friends and fellow-mandarins in the interior, and they to their literary companions and subordinates, who have never met the " foreign devil," who is painted to them as a monster of ignorance, ferocity, and vice; one whom they should dread and defend their country against. This is but an effort on the part of the mandarins at self-protection. As soon as foreigners are allowed to enter the country at will, railroads are introduced, communication becomes more rapid, and information more general as to how Western nations are governed, there will be an upheaval of existing government, and the mandarins will have to go. His days are numbered; he feels his end approaching, he struggles to the last to uphold the existing order of things, but he struggles in vain. Mandarin authority, as it now exists, resembling a decayed state of feudalism more than anything else, is doomed. There are some among the mandarin class who realize what a benefit free traffic with foreign nations and means of rapid interprovincial transportation would be to the nation, even though it should change the existing form of government. but who are willing, from patriotic motives, to make the advance and take the consequences; such are at present in the minority.

The fact is, however, becoming impressed upon the mandarin body, that, if they desire to see China remain under Chinese government at all, they will be obliged to keep foreign powers at bay by means of foreign engines and utensils of war. The uselessness of bows and arrows against repeating-rifles, of wooden junks against steel cruisers, is manifest. The necessity for more rapid means of transportation for troops and provisions in case of war than is possible with the clumsy conveyances now used is apparent to all. Yet, in the face of this knowledge, and with invasion by England, France, or Russia a possibility but too likely to be realized, these mandarins, from motives of selfishness, will fritter away their day of grace, and wake up to the necessity of meeting a war with a powerful nation without any means of defense.

Men they have in abundance, capable of making as good soldiers as any nation under heaven; and, properly armed, equipped, and officered, I would not be afraid to lead a regiment of Chinamen against one of any nationality of the earth. But what can the most courageous men do when armed with match-locks, spears, bows and arrows, or, perhaps, old muskets? They meet trained foes armed to the teeth with repeating-rifles, bayonets, and revolvers. There is but one result possible—overthrow and defeat. There are three great problems facing the Chinese people for solution, important in the order named, viz., preparation for national defense, suppression of opium traffic, and control of the Yellow River. How they will manage them is the subject of much speculation amongst those who are watching with intense interest the progress of this ancient nation.

Some desultory efforts have been made to put the nation in a condition of defense, as was manifest in their purchase and armament of the Chinese fleet. But we have, in the recent dismissal of Admiral Lang, through the jealousy of his Chinese subordinates, another proof of the sacrifice of patriotism and good of the country to personal selfishness and love of gain. Some of the troops have been armed with breech-loading rifles, and foreign drill-masters have spasmodically been employed to instruct a few regiments in tactics. But all that has been done so far is but as a drop in the bucket toward national defense. Owing to the unfortunate system in vogue, every contract given by a mandarin for the purchase of arms or ammunition is but a job out of which he gets a squeeze. His subordinates follow his example, and the common soldier imitates his superior by stealing and selling the powder given him to load for target-practice or entrusted to him as commissary. Although gunpowder is prohibited as an article of sale, yet, in the

Sons of General Chang Kao Yuan.

vicinity of any military camp, you can procure powder for twenty cents a pound that was bought in England or the United States by the Chinese government for fifty cents or over, showing conclusively that it is stolen and sold secretly by the soldiers or sub-officers. Indeed, one of them who knew I was fond of gunning, offered to procure as much for me as I wished at a very low price, but, knowing whence he would get it, I declined his offer. From the highest to the lowest, bribery and squeezing are regularly adopted as proper modes of obtaining position and wealth, and the Chinese political condition may be summed up in the one word,—corruption.

This is exactly the state of affairs Mencius two thousand years ago said would occur if the king, great men, scholars, and generals were each concerned only in profiting himself, viz., the kingdom would go to ruin.

Having reviewed at some length the condition of the governing powers, let us survey the borders of this ample domain and find out with whom China is most likely to come in collision. Stretching from the ninety-sixth to the one hundred and twentieth meridian of longitude east of Greenwich we find the northern boundary, being from the extreme western border of Kan Su to the extreme eastern border of Chih Li. (This does not include the province of Liao Tung, northeast of Chih Li, which is more of a territory under Chinese government than a province.) Along this whole northern boundary is Mongolia, nominally under Chinese control, but really under no control at all, being the dwelling of nomadic Mongol chiefs who roam about as they please and acknowledge no ruler. North of this neutral region, or all north of the forty-fourth parallel of latitude, is Russian Siberia;

so that Russia may be considered China's neighbor on the north. East of Liao Tüng, or Manchuria, is Korea; south of Korea the Yellow and Eastern Seas form the east boundary of China. The southern boundary is formed by the China Sea, the Gulf of Tonquin, the province of Annam, and British Burmah; the west, by Thibet and Ko Ko Nor, nominally Chinese possessions. The British, too, possess the island of Hong Kong, on the southern coast of China, and keep a well-trained garrison of English soldiers there at all times to defend their interests. It is only within the last few years that England has captured Burmah, and thus become one of China's immediate neighbors, and now there is constant report of trouble between the Burmese and Yunnanese, the province of China adjoining Burmah. This means that the next extension of British territory will be the territory of Yunnan, which is reported rich in mineral wealth and undeveloped mines. Great Britain is a great developer and takes a friendly interest in most countries of the globe, excepting Russia.

France has obtained a footing and established a colony in Tong King, which last reports say is flourishing, in spite of continual attacks of Annamese-Chinese pirates, and, doubtless, means to extend her possessions when a justifiable *casus belli* presents itself. Russia, on the north, has been building a railroad across Siberia the past two years or more, ever since she concluded it would be too expensive to wrest India from England by the northern route. This railroad is to be a developer of Siberia, not, of course, to transport troops to the northern frontier of China; and yet it might, on a pinch, be used for that purpose very well. In the meantime, Russian agents are weakening the Chinese influence in

Korea, and have succeeded so well that, whereas formerly Korea was an acknowledged dependency of China, now she is entirely independent, and is recognized as such by the United States, Great Britain, and Russia. Every one knows that for many years Russia has been trying to acquire an open-winter sea-port, and, up to the present, has signally failed; but the time is drawing near when she will make another effort, and, unless checkmated by some more important power than China, will obtain what she wants. China might protect herself from France, but against England or Russia she has very little show. It is likely, in event of Russia declaring war, that England would offer her assistance, but the Chinese who have discussed the matter with me appear to think they would rather fight it out alone than pay for England's assistance. Menaced with loss of territory from her three powerful neighbors, the Celestial Empire seems benumbed, and is making no adequate preparation for the struggle that may terminate her existence, or, at least, materially diminish her domain.

The occurrence of riots at many of the sea-port and inland cities during the past two or three years, directed against not only missionaries, but all foreigners, is at last arousing the attention from the powers of the world that it should have done much earlier. The murders of Messrs. Argent and Grant, with the menace of the foreign communities of Nanking and Hankow, have at last opened the eyes of the ministers, who are supposed to represent Great Britain and the United States, to dangers which have long been represented to them as certain to follow their policy of dealing with outrages against natives of the countries they represent. The combined protest of the diplomatic body in Peking has resulted in the following proclamation of the Tsung Li Yamen being received by the State Department:—

"The Tsung Li Yamen (or Council of Ministers) has memorialized us in regard to the missionary cases that have occurred in the various provinces, asking that we issue stringent instructions to the Governor-General and Governors to lose no time in devising means for a settlement thereof. It is represented by the Yamen that, in the month of May, the missionary premises (Catholic) at Wuhu, in the province of An Hui, were fired and destroyed by a mob of outlaws. At Tan Yang Huen, in the province of Kiang Su, and at Wusuchi, in the province of Hupeh, similar outrages have been committed in missionary establishments there, and it is now necessary that the miscreants should be arrested and unrelenting measures taken in good time to provide against further outrages of this kind. The propagation of Christianity by foreigners is provided for by treaty, and imperial decrees have been issued to the provincial authorities to protect the missionaries from time to time.

"For years peace and quiet have prevailed between Chinese and foreigners. How is it that recently there have been several missionary establishments burnt out and destroyed, and all happening at about the same time? This is decidedly strange and incredible. It is evident that among the rioters there are some powerful outlaws, whose object is to secretly contrive and plan to fan discontent among the people by circulating false rumors and causing them to become agitated and excited, and then to avail themselves of the opportunity to rob and plunder; and peaceable and law-abiding persons are enticed and led to join them, resulting in a tremendous uprising. If strenuous action is not taken to punish the miscreants, how can the majesty and dignity of the law be maintained, and peace and quiet prevail? Let the Governor-General and Governors of the Liang Kiang, Hu Kwang, Kiang Su, An Hui, and Hupeh issue, without delay, orders to the civil and military officers under their respective jurisdictions to cause the arrest of the leaders of the riots, try them, and inflict capital punishment upon them as a warning and example to others in the future. The doctrine of Christianity has for its purpose the teaching of men to be good. Chinese converts are subjects of China, and amenable to the local authorities.

" Peace and quiet should reign among the Chinese and missionaries. But there are reckless fellows, who fabricate stories, that have no foundation in fact, for the purpose of creating trouble. Villains of this class are not few in number, and are to be found everywhere. Let the Tartar generals, Governor-General, and Governors issue proclamations warning the people not to listen to idle rumors or false reports, which lead to trouble. Should any person secretly post placards containing false rumors, with a view to beguile the minds of the people, strenuous steps must be taken to cause his arrest, and vigorous punishment be meted out to him. The local authorities must protect the lives and property of foreign merchants and missionaries, and prevent bad characters from doing them injury.

" Should it transpire that the measures taken to protect them have not been adequate, and trouble, in consequence, ensues, the names of those officers who have been truly negligent are to be reported to us for degradation. In the matter of all missionary cases that are still pending, let the Tartar generals, Governor-General, and Governors cause a speedy settlement of them. They must not listen to the representations of their subordinates that the cases are difficult to settle, and thus cause delay, to the end that a settlement of them may be effected. Let this decree be universally promulgated for the information of the people."

This proclamation, if carried into effect, would speedily cause the disappearance of these periodically recurrent riots, and with them a danger to the peace of the country. But the likelihood of this proclamation being generally published all over the empire, and carried out to the letter, is small, if we may judge by previous experience. The more probable view is, that it was issued to please the foreign ambassadors in Peking, to quiet their outcry, and that, having accomplished its purpose, it will be like many former proclamations,—a dead-letter. If the Foreign Ministers' combination mean business, let them see that this proclamation, which is sufficiently sweeping, is published in every village of size throughout the empire, and that the first infringements of its text be punished to the extreme penalty.

CHAPTER XIII.

CHINA is greatly overcrowded. The struggle for existence is severe; the ground is tilled to the best advantage, even to the tops of the mountains, and yet thousands starve annually. The remedy for this state of affairs would seem to be emigration, or the production of commercial commodities, enabling the producers to purchase from abroad the food-supply necessary to make up the home deficiency. The Chinese are a home-loving people, and are not fond of mixing with other races. The great number who have emigrated to the United States, the Hawaiian Isles, Siam, and Australia have done so because a livelihood was denied them in their native country.

The Hawaiian Islands are fast becoming peopled by the Asiatic, and will doubtless soon be under their control. The United States and Australia having passed restrictive acts, they are pouring in great numbers into Siam, and already have charge of the principal business interests of that country. Singapore and the Straits Settlements are filled with them. British America and Mexico are receiving them in constantly-increasing numbers, and will doubtless, sooner or later, prohibit their entry. South American States have so far received but a small contingent of this tide of emigration, and, as the territory is large and the country sparsely populated, could accommodate vast numbers of the surplus of the flowery kingdom.

They need not, however, leave their own continent

(205)

if they only knew it. So far, almost the entire emigration has been from the extreme South, from the province of Kuang Tung, in the vicinity of the city of Canton; consequently, emigration by water has been cheaper and more convenient than overland without the facilities of rapid travel. To the North of the eighteen provinces the whole of Mongolia, nominally under Chinese control, and but sparsely populated, with its thousands of square miles of fine soil and temperate climate, would seem to offer a much more inviting home to the Chinaman forced to leave his birthplace than to emigrate to a foreign country, cross the dreaded ocean, and live among an alien race. The reasons why they do not accept it are: First, they are ignorant that there is any such country, and, second, the expense of getting there would make the attempt impossible.

An educated Chinaman with a purely native education knows very little of the geography of his native land, and the mass of the people do not know the names of the eighteen provinces, nor what is their relative position. True, nearly every one knows there are eighteen provinces, for one of the native names for China is "Shih Pa Sheng," the eighteen provinces. But ask a man the names of the eighteen, and, if an ordinary farmer, he will not be able to tell you more than three.

If the Chinese government were more wide awake to its duty in caring for its people, and at the same time its opportunity of preparing for national defense, it would assist the surplus population of the eighteen provinces to remove to, and settle in, the Mongolian territory alluded to, and thus furnish an additional barrier to Russian invasion. Nothing so far has been done in this direction, or seems likely to be, for the reason that the importance of the condition of the country is always secondary to private ambition; and it is likely to remain so until too late. So that emigration as a relief to the surplus population seems likely to pursue in the future the same course as in the past, viz., an individual will go to the country by water where reports say work is to be obtained, and to which means of transportation are cheapest.

As to production, the policy of the government is the same. Mines are the property of the crown, and are not allowed to be worked by private individuals. Manufactures, owing to absence of native iron and coal mines, and to restriction of foreigners doing business in the interior, are impossible; and so, large numbers of people who might have lucrative employment are, by the policy of the government, kept in idleness and poverty. How long this ancient and imbecile policy will continue no one can safely prophecy, and it is to this uncertainty that estimates of the future of the country owe lack of definiteness.

In the works of Mencius, one of the old kings, in talking to the philosopher, said, "When the year is bad and the crops fail on the inside of the river, I move the people to the outside (or a portion of them), and carry grain to those remaining; when it is bad on the outside I follow the reverse plan; thus do all my people have peace and plenty, and the State is preserved." If the Emperor of to-day would follow the same plan he would insure the preservation of his empire and the affection of his people. I have heard repeated, on many occasions, the remark, " The present dynasty cannot long endure; there is too much misery." A change of dynasty is not necessary, nor would it likely be beneficial. A change of policy is wanted. A change that will recognize the happiness and prosperity of the people as the best means of preserving the empire.

The conservation of an empire or republic depends upon a satisfied condition of its people with their form of government and its ability to defend its frontiers. Although the people of China cannot be said to be entirely satisfied with the present order of things, still they have endured, and would endure it, if let alone, indefinitely. The entrance upon the scene of foreigners, by enlightening the people, is, however, causing more and more dissatisfaction, and what is now simply grumbling and murmurs of discontent among the populace may, in time, become rebellion. If such a thing were possible that China should expel and never re-admit foreigners, the country would doubtless remain unchanged for another thousand years. Foreigners, however, have come to stay, and continue to come in increasing numbers, and, despite the objection and obstructive policy of the government, are steadily gaining ground with this nation of born traders. The increase in native population and wealth at the sea-port cities is proof at a glance of what foreign intercourse would do for the interior cities, now falling to ruins, if permitted. The people of the interior are slowly awakening to this fact, and it serves to increase their discontent. Not that they want the foreigner, but they want the means of prosperity.

Riots in the interior against the missionaries, and even in some cases against foreign Customs' officials in Chinese employ, are the outcome of agitation stirred up by the mandarins and literary men disappointed in obtaining office, who seek in this way to stir up the people against the existing government and effect a change. These riots have become more and more frequent in the past few years, owing to the mild manner of Western powers in dealing with the Chinese. No other nation has been allowed to maltreat German, English, Italian, French, and American citizens or subjects, and then take two or three years to pay a trifling indemnity. It is scarcely to be wondered at that many of the Chinese, even mandarins, think the world afraid of China. One reason for this lack of protection on the part of the powers is a general feeling of unconcern for the missionaries. It is felt that they need not expose themselves in places known to be hostile, and that, when they do, they only get what they deserve when they are beaten or mobbed and their residences looted.

While it is true that in many instances missionaries might avoid trouble by the exercise of more prudence, yet, as long as the United States and other powers, by treaty stipulations, have maintained their right to travel and preach in the interior, it is the duty of the governments, native and foreign, to protect them. Usually more or less of an indemnity is tardily paid, but never are the ringleaders brought to justice. This rioting, becoming more frequent each year, will soon lead to complications that will involve the Chinese government in a war with one or more of the powers, whose subjects are maltreated without provocation. Though much enduring and patient, this state of affairs cannot last indefinitely.

As to the ability of China to defend her borders, neither upon land or sea is she prepared to meet the trained forces of any foreign power. Her soldiers do not lack in bravery, but in discipline and equipment.

Many native regiments are armed with rusty spears only, or with matchlocks. Some have old smooth-bore, muzzle-loading muskets, and a few are armed with breech-loading rifles. No adequate commissary department exists, and in time of war the peasantry would be at the mercy of the soldiery, who would be compelled to take provisions where they could be found. The Chinese navy is in some respects better off than the army, having a number of fine modern cruisers, bought of late years from European contractors; but as yet they have not been able to navigate them without foreign assistance, and, were they deprived of their foreign instructors, would soon wreck them or ruin them by neglect. The country is taxed as heavily as it can well stand, but the taxes, unfortunately, do not find their way into the imperial treasury until they have been greatly reduced by official squeezes.

The first abuse which needs attention in a reconstructive policy of government, to place the finances in a sound state, would be to stop this enormous leak. How it could be done I will not suggest. That it can be done by Chinese officials I do not affirm, but that it would be done were a foreign protectorate established I am certain. With the revenue increased, useless expenditures stopped, and a just and patriotic policy adopted by those in power, the country could, within a few years, be placed in a condition for defense that would defy the attacks of any power, no matter how strong.

The construction of trunk lines of railroads for transportation of troops and provisions would give employment to thousands of discontented laborers. Public arsenals, foundries, and machine-shops would give the people confidence in the power of their country, and by

this means increase their patriotism and courage. No adequate coast defenses exist. This demands the labor of thousands to accomplish, and affords work for the miner, the mason, and the mechanic, to say nothing of the unskilled laborer.

China is able to take her place amongst the foremost powers of the earth, if she would only realize her present position and rise to meet the emergency. Pursuing the same policy as she has for hundreds of years, she seems nearly oblivious of the existence of new times demanding different policy. Her people are slowly becoming enlightened as to the condition of foreign powers, and to the helplessness of their own country. Let chose in power take warning and place their country in a more honorable position than at the tail of civilization, or some others will do it for them. The resources of the country cannot be accurately known, but enough is known to be certain that the precious minerals, iron, and coal are to be had in abundance for the mining, and the soil is good all over the country for agricultural purposes. The enormous population affords material for an army that could discount that of any European power, but in the present state of the exchequer they could neither be armed nor equipped.

The safety of China thus far has lain in the fact that the powers of the world have been too engaged elsewhere to pay her much attention; but now, with the peace of Europe tolerably well assured, it is by no means certain that the Celestial Empire will be allowed to pursue the even tenor of her way, to the exclusion of the interests of the rest of the world. It is next to a certainty that Russia is determind to have a Southern sea-port. Whether Korea will answer her purpose or not remains to be seen, but, in the opinion of those who have considered this question from the outside, the probability is that Russia does not want Korea; at least, not at present.

A few years ago it was very amusing to hear of a Russian fleet sailing to a port on the Chinese, Japanese, or Korean coast, and then hearing of an English fleet being ordered to the same point. England is very jealous of the Russian interest in Korea, and is trying by every means in her power to prevent any concessions to that country. But one thing is certain: England cannot prevent the construction of the Trans-Siberian railway; nor, when it is completed, can she interfere with a Russo-Chinese war, except by an alliance with China, which at present there is no likelihood of China accepting. Should an alliance with China be formed, the whole of Europe would be drawn into the conflict, and war such as has never been known be the result. It is to be sincerely hoped that no such train of circumstances will come to pass.

Let us hope and believe that China's rulers will awaken to their duty, for patriotism's sake drop their internal jealousies, and hasten to develop all the latent industries of their country. Rouse, oh, ye mandarins! Awake, oh, ye that rule! Open mines, build foundries, construct railroads, erect forts, arm and equip your soldiers, educate yourselves and your people, and your country is safe! Sleep on a little longer, import more of the deadly drug that is benumbing your energies, and, when you have passed away, not your sons but an alien will rule. Take your choice—which?